Hungarian Rhapsody

An Adoption Story

James Derk

To Mary –
Thank you for your love +
support of my Dad all these
years.
Best,
Jim

Bloomington, IN Milton Keynes, UK

authorHOUSE®

AuthorHouse™
1663 Liberty Drive, Suite 200
Bloomington, IN 47403
www.authorhouse.com
Phone: 1-800-839-8640

AuthorHouse™ UK Ltd.
500 Avebury Boulevard
Central Milton Keynes, MK9 2BE
www.authorhouse.co.uk
Phone: 08001974150

First published by AuthorHouse 10/4/2006

ISBN: 1-4259-5712-9 (sc)
ISBN: 1-4259-5713-7 (dj)

Printed in the United States of America
Bloomington, Indiana

This book is printed on acid-free paper.

Photographs by James Derk © 2006
Family portraits by Heather Lucas, Click Photography, Evansville, Indiana

For Kimberly,
My best friend and
co-pilot in this nutty adventure

No Day But Today

Hungarian Rhapsody:

An Adoption Story

INTRODUCTION

By the time my wife, Kimberly, and I got married on a windswept beach on Maui in 1995, we had already agreed we wanted to have children. Even though I was almost 35 by then and though we each had one child from our first marriages, we were ready to build a larger family.

Like most everything else, we approached this decision with a detailed plan. Because we'd both battled infertility issues in the past, we decided to pursue both infertility treatments and adoption simultaneously and go with whatever option produced fruit first.

On the infertility side, we worked with a respected fertility doctor in Indiana who assured us we'd have no trouble conceiving. With fingers crossed and wallets open we started down an expensive course of surgeries, bizarre fertility drugs and in-vitro treatments. After blowing through $60,000 (not covered by our health insurance) we threw in the towel on science and fully focused our efforts on adoption.

Neither of us had to be "talked into" adoption in the first place, and we didn't view it as a "second choice." I had already adopted my son in my first marriage; Kim's dad was adopted, and my sister had adopted a baby girl and was working on a second. Our only real decision was where to find the child or two to complete our family.

We looked into adopting several siblings from our home state of Indiana but quickly grew frustrated with the bureaucracy, especially when we tried to adopt biracial children. (Rules put into place in 2001 made domestic adoption much easier than when we were first looking. There's now one Web site, www. adoptuskids.org, where prospective adoptive parents can find children from all over the country who need a loving home.) However, back then it was a lot of searching county by county and a lot of dead-ends.

We turned to other areas, and found a local attorney had developed a fledgling adoption program from Bolivia. After several meetings with him we signed up and got very excited as we got in line with a few other couples that were also going to make the trip to the exotic mountains of La Paz.

However, military unrest in Bolivia made our adoption dreams there pretty unlikely in our one-year timeframe. (Our paperwork, including an expensive home study, was only good for 12 months. If we could not complete the process in that period, we'd have to have another updated study, and we frankly couldn't afford it after all of our infertility bills.) As our adoption paperwork got ready to expire, we turned to other countries in desperation.

That's when Kim, searching the Internet one day, found a Web page about some children in Hungary looking for a home. From there our adventure began.

Some of the text in the following pages comes direct from our e-mails sent home at the time. Some is adapted from an award-winning series of stories I wrote for *The Evansville Courier & Press* newspaper, where I was working as an editor.

Both Kim and I were trained as journalists, and we kept pretty extensive notes at the time, partly to share with our kids and partly to keep our sanity as the strange world of adoption swirled around us.

We hope that sharing our story, warts and all, may shed some light on the murky world of international adoption, encourage others to consider it, and give at least one more child a forever family.

CHAPTER 1: The Beginning

Everyone thought we had lost our minds.

Going overseas to adopt one child is stressful; our plan to head to Hungary and bring back four kids at once seemed impossible. Little did we know then our adoption journey would not stop with only four.

There have been moments in the last few years when my wife, Kimberly, and I have questioned our sanity. But we've never questioned our decision to make a home for Kristian, 4, William, 3, and 1-year-old twins Ava and Adam, then a year later tiny Cary, age 18 months, and then later even tinier Kristiana, age 14 months.

Their arrival has changed virtually everything about our lives.

While battling infertility with significant amounts of dollars and emotions — and losing — we turned to adoption with open eyes. We initially hoped to adopt an infant and a toddler but really had no requirements or expectations other than trying to complete the process with as little hassle as possible. We were just hoping to welcome the thunder of little feet in the house.

We just didn't quite expect 12 new feet at once.

Our children from our previous marriages, Kim's 17-year-old daughter, Coleen, and my 6-year-old son, Brandon, (also adopted, from the USA) supported us in our decision so that part was easy.

What wasn't easy was making it through the bureaucracy involved in finding and arranging for the adoptions. We initially asked about three siblings we'd heard about in Indiana, but another couple applied before we did. We were turned down for another trio because of issues about our race versus the race of the kids.

We then heard about a program in Evansville, Indiana, to adopt children from Bolivia and eagerly applied.

But in 1996, after giving the Bolivians a year to get their act together, we started looking at other countries because our expensive home-study paperwork was about to expire.

Kim's employer, General Electric, had an adoption-assistance program available for its employees, and caseworkers there began to offer us alternatives. China was out because we already had children and it had rules in place that made it hard to adopt if you already had kids. Russia was possible, as were Guatemala, Ethiopia, Mexico, and Romania.

While researching those countries, we also turned to the Internet for help. One day Kim discovered a Web page about a sibling group of four from Hungary. The children's information was placed on the Web in desperation after the Hungarian government tried for months to find some family in Hungary or Europe willing to keep all four siblings together.

We sat down on the couch and looked over the basic information provided. All we knew about the children were their ages and some made-up names (the children were called *Fred Flintstone, Barney Rubble and Pebbles and Bam-Bam.*) To protect their privacy, there were no photos of the kids posted online.

We talked it over.

In rational terms, adopting four children at once made no sense. Our house in Indiana, built by Kim's grandparents, was way too small for four more kids. With adoption costs running $15,000 to $20,000 per child, we couldn't come close to affording it. (We hadn't even come close to paying off the infertility treatments.) We didn't have a van big enough to haul everyone around. Leaving our jobs for a month to live in Hungary (the residency requirement in that country) would be a huge hardship. The children wouldn't speak English. And our daily budget would have big trouble handling four more kids — three in diapers — with Kim's daughter, Coleen, heading to Purdue University in a year.

If we did somehow pull it off and go massively into debt, we knew neither of us could quit our full-time jobs and stay home with the kids, something we really wanted to do. So that meant significant day-care expenses and other logistical hassles. Then there was the parenting aspect: did we really have it in us?

We talked about it for hours, both the pros and the cons. On paper the cons outweighed the pros by about 20 to 1. But for some reason these children, though faceless and nameless, had clambered into our hearts.

The next morning we faxed our adoptive home study to Hungary and asked if we could bring all four children home to Indiana. As the last piece of paper disappeared into the fax machine, we prayed that whoever was receiving the document on the other end would grant us our request.

The next process would be the publishing of our names and the names of the children on a Hungarian National Register (basically to give people a chance to protest) and the close examination of our financial records and home study.

Our financial bind got some help when President Bill Clinton signed a new law giving a $5,000 tax credit for every child adopted in 1997 and beyond. It wouldn't pay all the bills, but $20,000 sure would help.

There's no way we could handle all of the red tape ourselves, so we hired a Hungarian adoption "facilitator," also found on the Internet. János Samu would help us through the bureaucratic maze involved in a foreign adoption and work as an interpreter for us.

He'd meet us in Hungary for the first week, get the process rolling, and then return to the States. We'd be on our own for another three weeks while the paperwork wound through the Hungarian system.

Once we got the approvals from the court, we'd have to apply to the American Embassy in Budapest for visas so the children could enter the United States as our dependents. If that was approved, we could take our children out of the orphanage and into a world they'd never seen.

While we were waiting, we received a photocopy of photos of the four children. Kristian was tall, thin and blond. He stood clutching a plastic toy

3

of a spaceship and looked a little curious. Willie looked about as big as his brother, but had a mischievous grin on his face.

The twins, Adam and Ava, were lying on their backs, staring at the camera. They looked nearly identical and strongly resembled their older brothers.

Kim and I took turns staring at the photos, trying to find some hints to their personality, some clues in their eyes that they were doing all right.

Waiting for the decision from the Hungarian orphanage directors was a nightmare. If they said no, we'd be crushed. If they said yes, we'd have two weeks' notice to leave the country, find a way to stay in Hungary for a month, then eventually return with four children.

We had some jitters to be sure, especially when the universal refrain from everyone we told was: "Are you nuts?" But somehow we were at peace with our decision and our plan.

We took a deep breath and plunged in, headfirst.

CHAPTER 2: Where's Hungary?

After we faxed to Hungary our initial papers requesting permission to adopt the children, we had to wait for a preliminary decision. Kim and I fretted for days about what would happen if we were turned down.

Though we knew them only from a few photos and brief descriptions, these four siblings had become *our* children. We couldn't bear the thought of having something go wrong now.

We already were shell-shocked from repeated delays from our earlier attempts to adopt from Bolivia and were way out of our element in dealing with foreign governments.

While we waited, we called our local caseworker from Catholic Charities to update our home study for four children. (We previously had been approved for a maximum of two.) Her response "Four? Are you sure?"

She took another look at our finances and agreed that we could handle it (compared to average Hungarians we were the Rockefellers). We sent our caseworker some flowers, faxed the double-notarized revision to Hungary and hoped it would help us get a positive answer.

Quick.

We then called our parents and extended family and found almost universal acceptance, tempered by an understandable concern regarding if we could handle everything. Coleen, Kim's daughter, was fully supportive, and Brandon was very keen on having some other kids in the house as long as he remained the oldest of the little kids. (Kim and I both had agreed to scotch the deal if either child had concerns.)

Our adoption facilitator, János, was an American citizen born in Hungary who led a life of adventure novels. He was imprisoned for a year by the Russians for the "crime" of trying to leave Hungary with his wife on a forged passport. He and his family eventually got out of occupied Hungary in 1973 on another forged passport. He opened up a translation company, East-West Concepts Inc., and has been in love with language ever since. You have to like a man who can speak a couple dozen languages (including *Dzongkha*) and has 2,000 dictionaries in his office.

Since the country became free after the Berlin Wall fell in 1989 (the Russians had occupied Hungary after World War II and conveniently had forgotten to leave) János had helped dozens of couples through the maze of Hungarian adoption. He made some phone calls to Hungarian officials on our behalf, and his efforts quickly paid off. Within days we received the amazing news that we were fully approved and should come to Hungary "as soon as possible."

A court date was set in a mere two weeks.

Our joy was tempered only by the amount of work we had to do at home to get ready.

Kim and I knew we had to learn all we could about Hungary and its people. (I literally had to go find a globe in Brandon's room and look up where Hungary sat on the Earth.) My father toured Chicago's bookstores and sent us half-dozen books on the country and language, which we devoured.

We read that Hungary is a republic about the size of Indiana that is home to about 10 million people, many of whom are low-income service workers. The orphanage where our children lived was in Debrecen, a city of 212,000 in eastern Hungary, about a three-hour drive from Budapest and quite near the Romanian border.

We quickly gave up on learning any major portion of the Hungarian language after reading it was one of the hardest languages for English-speakers to learn. Hungarian has 35 cases (forms of nouns according to whether it is subject, object, etc.) and we were not about to pick that up in a couple of weeks with Berlitz tapes.

I called one of our local colleges, the University of Evansville, hoping someone from Hungary might be studying here on some sort of exchange program. They connected me with two students from neighboring Romania and one student from Ireland who had worked in a Romanian orphanage. When I quickly asked why two Romanians would be any help for us, I learned a portion of Romania had once been part of the empire of Hungary, and residents of that portion of Romania still speak Hungarian.

We took the students, Anna Gyongyossy, Adel Lorinc and Gareth Blayney, to dinner and tried our best to learn more of the culture of the country we'd call home for a month.

We knew we were in trouble when they told us the word "szia" (pronounced "see-ya") meant hello and the word "hello" meant "goodbye."

We were told Hungarians generally like Americans, with a bit of envy (and sometimes resentment) for our standard of living. Much of Hungary's current popular culture is based on American icons such as Levis and Nikes, which few can afford.

In 1997, a skilled worker in Hungary could expect to earn about $100 to $200 a month working about 12-hour days with few days off. Inflation periodically ravages the economy, hitting a staggering 31 percent in 1995. About 4 percent of the people (but most of the orphans) are Roma. Formerly called "Gypsies," Roma are soundly discriminated against in Europe.

(Early on the orphanage officials hurriedly assured us our children were not Roma, as if it were some medical ailment. "It's no problem if they are," Kim told them to puzzled stares. "Why would it matter?")

Hungary as a country stands out as completing very few American adoptions. In 1997, the country completed six adoptions by Americans (four of them were ours); by 2003 it had only risen to 16. Compare that to more than 1,000 for China or 250 from Haiti.

To its credit, Hungary has a strong protection system for children, much better than America's. After every birth, we were told, the mother remains in the hospital for several days. During that time, a caseworker goes to the parents' home and determines if it is fit for children.

If not, the child is taken to the "infants' home," (a.k.a. the orphanage) where the parents and other family members can visit and where the child will remain (for free) until living conditions at home improve. If conditions never improve, but if the family continues to have contact with the child at least every six months, the parental rights are maintained. The child continues to live in the institution, however.

If the parents don't maintain contact and six months pass, the orphanage contacts the parents and family. If no one wants the children and another six months pass, the children can be considered "orphans" and adoptable by others.

Though we weren't told specifics at that point, we figured that's what happened to our four. We were told both parents were suffering from mental illnesses, which were variously described to us as schizophrenia, psychosis and other terms. We discussed this at some depth with our doctors; we knew that some mental illnesses were genetic and we were rolling a bit of a dice here. But we really didn't care. If the children were mentally fine, then great. If not, then surely the United States was a better place to deal with it than a Hungarian orphanage. So we pressed ahead.

The oldest, Kristian, 4, had been in the infants' home since he was 6 months old; the other three were taken there directly from the hospital after their births.

We were very curious about their background and their medical condition but by then we didn't really care when they got there, how or why. Our goal was to get them out of there as fast as we could and home to a loving environment.

Doing that would prove a lot more difficult than we expected.

CHAPTER 3: Plans are made

"You want a loan for *what*?"

The loan officer's confusion was understandable. How many times does a couple walk into a bank branch and ask for a loan — *immediately* — so they can adopt four children?

Part of the problem was that Kim and I really had no idea what our adoption adventure in Hungary would cost. We guessed high at $50,000 and figured we could always return the leftover funds when we got back.

As the bank worked on our loan application, we were busy making plans.

The first step was to keep our jobs. Though Kimberly had worked for GE Plastics only for about six months, her company treated her like gold. My bosses at *The Evansville Courier & Press* newspaper, where I was then city editor, were less than enthusiastic about me being gone for a whole month given my role in the newsroom. However, I had worked there for 15 years and had enough vacation time saved up to make it close enough.

We then headed to the airlines. We didn't have the 30-day advance purchase window for a really cheap ticket; heck we didn't even have two weeks' notice. The most efficient way to getting to Hungary was via Malev, the Hungarian national airline. Tickets set us back $1,500 each because we had not been able to book in advance.

Because of the cost we also tentatively booked one-way return tickets for the older boys and decided we'd hold the twins on our laps. That would save at least $3,000, a move we'd regret later.

That left our too-small house. We had neither the time nor money to add on, but we desperately wanted the kids to come home to a place they could call their own instead of being stuffed into a small space. We figured they'd had enough of confined spaces to last a lifetime.

We decided to gut our walkout basement and build bedrooms for the two older boys and the twins downstairs. It wouldn't cost that much but would make a significant difference in our house. Because we wanted to be on the same floor as the kids, our plan was to use the former family room downstairs for a master bedroom and build a large suite for the boys with two sets of bunk beds and a bathroom. A smaller room for the twins (with two cribs) would be attached to that.

We hired a contractor and hoped for the best, knowing most of the work would have to be done while we were overseas.

Kim's parents offered to leave their home near Cincinnati to live at our house while we were gone, supervising the construction and caring for Belle, our main dog, and Ginger, our backup, auxiliary dog.

The last two weeks before we left were a blur of bank applications, passport photos, immigration documents, inoculations, and drywall dust.

The paperwork aspect of any adoption is a nightmare; but throw in anything involving the U.S. Immigration and Naturalization Service and you enter a whole new level of bureaucratic nonsense. At one point, INS officials nearly scotched the whole deal because Kim's fingerprints weren't "dark enough" and because we had mistakenly filed INS Form I-600 and not I-600A.

(Working with the INS was the most frustrating part of our adoptions, by far. It's the only U.S. government agency I know where the state and local offices have unlisted phone numbers.)

We kept working at our jobs right up until the night before departure, mainly to earn precious money and save vacation days, but that meant a lot of nights where we stayed up until 2 a.m. getting everything packed and ready.

We really had no idea what to pack; we didn't even know whether the children would have clothes on their backs. Without knowing their sizes, we really had no choice but to pack very light and hope we could buy what we needed for them when we got over there.

Before we left, a friend, Beth Katz, invited Kim to a local support group for parents of multiple siblings. Group members showered her with support and advice.

When Kim came home that night, we sat in the kitchen surrounded by bags of donated clothes, shoes and toys.

"We can do this," she said.

And I believed her.

CHAPTER 4: On our way

Thanks to all of Kim's preparation we soon stood at the Evansville airport with four packed bags and an empty stroller. We boarded our tiny commuter plane and headed off on our international adventure.

Winging our way to Budapest, my wife and I could only wonder what we had forgotten to do and worry about what remained ahead.

Our facilitator, János, had handled most of the Hungarian paperwork for us, an immeasurable help. Knowing what papers to file and when is much of the headache in an international adoption. Although he'd never heard of another couple adopting four children at once, he assured us things would go relatively smoothly.

Our goal on this Sunday was to fly to Budapest, then rent a car and drive three hours to Debrecen in eastern Hungary. We were to meet our children for the first time the following day.

The 18-hour trip over was uneventful and went amazingly fast, despite three connections. It was our first trip overseas together and Kim and I were pretty excited about that, too.

When we landed we were literally dumped into a country where everything was new and we didn't have a prayer of communicating with anyone.

Because we hoped to be returning to the airport in a month with four children, I rented the largest car in the Hertz fleet — perhaps the largest car in the country — which turned out to be a Ford Mondeo. It was about the size of an American subcompact car and way too small. But I didn't have any other choices with the Hungarian clerk anyway. I kept using what I thought was the Hungarian word for "big," and he kept saying the Hungarian word for "yes."

We had no Hungarian money when we landed (the banks in Evansville laughed at my request for some in advance) so I headed to an airport ATM and inserted my card. I was confronted with a hilariously confusing Hungarian menu. I figured out the first screen (type in the PIN number) then was presented with a multiple-choice screen of how many Hungarian "Forints" I wanted. Deeply jet-lagged, I had completely forgotten even a close guess at the exchange rate. The fewest number of Forints allowed to be withdrawn was 1,000; the most was 50,000. Of course, not knowing if I was withdrawing enough for a newspaper or a mortgage, I hit "5,000" and held my breath.

Out came five 1,000-Forint bills, and we headed to the car armed with our Hungarian map. It was only when we stopped at a roadside store to buy a couple of Cokes did I realize I had withdrawn about 15 bucks from the ATM. As we headed back to the car with our "Cola" and "Cola Light" I realized I could not find the Ford's reverse gear. We sat there in the small parking lot like idiots as I ground the gears while passing locals stared at us.

We tried every switch and knob on the console before resorting to the owner's manual, printed in Hungarian and German. Kim's high school German classes apparently failed to include the word "reverse" as she was no help whatever until she found a photo that showed I had to lift a small piece of plastic on the shift knob to engage reverse.

We must have laughed for miles. (Kilometers?)

Zooming down Route 4, I soon realized that Eastern European drivers are both brazen and insane, a terrible combination. These little cars powered by tiny engines would pass us with inches (centimeters actually) to spare. I had no idea what the speed limit on the road was -- there were no signs -- so I generally just tried to keep up with the rest of the cars, buses, and huge trucks. Dozens of small white crosses dotted the side of the roadway marking where Hungarians had not quite made it back over the centerline.

Arriving in Debrecen, we drove around in circles for two hours trying to find the small hotel amid a cacophony of street signs. We eventually found the tiny Park Hotel hidden deep in Debrecen's "Great Forest."

"Who would hide a hotel?" I asked Kim. We later discovered the hotel was a former Soviet retreat used as a hunting lodge. Designed to be "bug-proof," it was hidden deep in the forest to conceal it from the Americans and their listening devices during the Cold War.

Our small room, one of a dozen in the small hotel, was richly wood-paneled, quite Spartan but very clean. A small TV spouting German programming sat in one corner after a staff member showed us how to turn it on.

The bed consisted of an upholstered wooden frame, plus a thin feather duvet and feather pillows, a major problem because of my avian allergies.

My attempt to get a foam pillow from the front desk clerk (using my thick Hungarian phrase book) produced our second laughing fit of the trip after the clerk knocked on the door an hour later and quizzically delivered a small pad from the patio furniture outside. For the duration of our stay there, the staff must have been abuzz about the pile of feather bedding in the corner and the two odd Americans who slept on the hard box spring with rolled-up towels for pillows.

Our hotel and its staff were a near-perfect mimic of the BBC-TV show "*Fawlty Towers*" except there was no Basil on duty... just a dozen Manuels.

That night we met János in person for the first time in the lobby of the small hotel. He looked just like I suspected he would; short and stocky, with a round face and the eyes of someone who had lived a life well-earned. We trusted him immediately; he seemed to know exactly what would happen at each step.

We sat in the small lobby discussing our visit to the orphanage the next morning. He warned us that the children probably would be hesitant about us at first. That went double for me, I was told, because men are hardly ever seen there and the kids may be afraid of me.

Though we were certain about completing the adoption already, the children were told only that they would have visitors, not anything about the visitors being prospective parents. We were horrified when János said they don't tell the children anything else in case the parents back out. As incredible as it sounds, a few couples had been known to travel halfway across the world, only to decide they do not like something about the child and fly back home.

János said he'd even seen the rejection happen over things like hair color or skin tone.

We could not imagine such a thing.

He told us our goal for the first meeting should be to try to play with the children at their pace and not push ourselves on them. We also were told not to tell the children we loved them; in Hungary that expression was reserved for adult romantic relationships.

(It was a rule we broke the next day.)

János also discussed what he had learned about the background of the children; Kristian had been in the infants' home since he was 6 months old; he had turned four that summer. William, who had just turned three a few days before, and the twins, Adam and Ava, who had just turned one, had been taken there directly from hospitals after their birth.

Kristian had been removed from his biological parents' home as a toddler following the death of his 2-½ year old sister, who had choked on a rubber ball. Investigators looking into that case had determined his biological parents could not properly care for Kris and removed him from the home after finding him malnourished and living in terrible conditions.

When Willie was born shortly thereafter, the welfare officials determined the household situation wasn't any better and put him in the same orphanage. Two years later, the same story with the twins, who were added to Willie's room.

The parents lost their parental rights because they quickly stopped visiting the children in the institution and didn't respond to the government's attempts to convince them to continue to visit and otherwise maintain contact.

We were told the parents both were classified as mentally ill; one with schizophrenia and one from "psychosis." We heard other words like "manic depression" and "substance abuse" but the problem with mental illness, we knew, is there are no definitive tests. Going in we knew something had to be mentally amiss with the birth parents anyway (who would give up their children and never look back?) and we were prepared to work on whatever the Lord gave us.

We asked more questions, but János said we'd learn more the next day from the orphanage director. He simply didn't know any more.

We went up to bed with dozens of unanswered questions but still unwavering in our decision. We didn't particularly care of the circumstances of how they got into the institution.

We just wanted them home.

The orphanage in Debrecen

CHAPTER 5: The meeting

We met János the next morning for what we hoped would be a quick breakfast at our hotel. Both Kim and I ordered Cokes, which was met with a quizzical glance from the waiter. When a swallow-sized bottle showed up, I ordered three more at once, earning me odd stares. (For the remainder of our stay, both Kim and I ordering Coke for breakfast provided immeasurable entertainment for the wait staff at various European eateries.)

To say we hurried through the meal would be a major understatement. We had absolutely no idea what to expect when we got to the orphanage. We'd only seen that one photo of each kid; we had no idea what they had been told about us. Did they even know we're coming that day? Would they know who we were? Did they even know what "parents" were? How would we even talk to them?

We were beyond surprised to find that the orphanage was just a short block from our hotel. We'd driven past it a dozen times while we were lost trying to find the hotel, but couldn't read the sign. I could have thrown a rock from the hotel parking lot and hit it.

The building itself was an unassuming concrete and stucco structure full of small rooms, much like a hospital in America from 1950. It looked very clean despite being home to about 200 children under age 4.

We met first with the orphanage director and other staff members in her spotless office. We were greeted warmly, with looks from all of the staff members, looks we later found out meant "I think they're nuts." We sat down, sipped tea from immaculate cups, and waited to hear the story of our children as various staff members made excuses to walk by the doorway to look at us.

The director took out a thick folder tied with an old shoestring and began to talk in rapid Hungarian. János did his best to translate as she went along.

We were shocked to find out that the 1-year-old twins, Adam and Ava, and Willie were living in one room with six other kids but that Kristian had been kept in another wing. He had never been told of his brothers and sister; he wasn't even aware he had siblings. This was very disappointing to us, as we had hoped Willie and Kris would have established a strong brotherly relationship. Turns out they had never even met.

When we asked why the siblings had not been placed together during their life here, the orphanage director looked up and told us simply: "We had no idea anyone would ever want all four." She smiled a little, and tears welled up in her eyes.

It made sense really; they didn't want to establish a bond that would have to be shattered if they were not placed together or, more likely, never adopted at all. We were told when we had first inquired about the adoption, Kris (and maybe Willie) had been only days from being sent away to another institute for older kids. Once sent there, they could not have been adopted without great difficulty.

We consider getting there in time the luckiest break of the entire adventure.

The staff had really been making an exception for Kristian, almost hiding him from the state officials to prevent him from being moved to the orphanage for older children. He should have been moved to the other place a year before, but staffers were holding out hope someone would come and take him home. He had become a staff favorite because of his wonderful disposition and personality.

We asked about the medical history of the children, expecting to find out very little. Amazingly the orphanage kept detailed files on every child, even down to listing every meal they'd ever eaten there. Medically, they claimed all of the kids checked out fine except Adam, who had been born with a persistent heart murmur. He had been very ill as an infant and hospitalized with some ailment for more than a month, but we didn't get any details then about what that might have been. As for the heart, a Hungarian cardiologist recommended follow-up care in the United States, which had infinitely better medical equipment.

We asked about the history of the parents and were told little. We found out that both were alive. The father worked as a laborer, perhaps a carpenter, and had a history of mental problems. The mother was about 30 years old and also had a long history of what they called schizophrenia and other issues.

When I asked the director, through János, to review the file and find something positive we could share with the kids later about their biological parents, the director visibly warmed to the question. She then slowly flipped through the folder for a few quiet minutes then simply, sadly, shook her head no and closed the book.

At the end of the interview, we were told we would have 48 hours after meeting the kids to formally accept or reject the adoption. Kim looked at me and then immediately replied that we had already made up our minds and wanted to sign the papers now.

With a shocked look, the director said the law required that we actually had to *meet* the children first. So we got up and began the long walk down several rather dark, winding halls with windowed rooms on one side.

As we passed each room, at least a half-dozen children ran to each window and door. Every room was seemingly packed with adorable kids, most with the dark, shiny hair typical of Roma toddlers. We waved and smiled, then felt the pangs of heartache as the rooms—and the kids—kept coming.

The children there were living in two-room units with about eight to 10 kids per unit. One room was a sleeping area and was filled with old metal cribs and small beds. The other room was a play area, with a few well-used toys, dolls and balls. A bathroom area with a small bathtub connected the two rooms.

Each room had a main caregiver and several other women who worked rotating shifts.

As we walked, it seemed all noise in the place simply stopped. The children ran to press their little faces against the glass windows of their rooms. I'll never forget the big, vacant eyes of the children as they watched us pass.

I kept hoping the next room would be ours. It felt so helpless seeing all of those children we could not take home. I just tried to smile and keep moving down the long halls.

Our kids, of course, ended up being in the last room in the last hall.

When we walked in, Kris and Willie were playing with small plastic toys; the babies, Adam and Ava, were sitting up in their cribs. Kris and Willie looked at us and dropped what they were doing. We dropped to our knees and Kris, prodded by his caregiver, ran over and gave each of us a big hug and a kiss on both cheeks. Willie immediately followed with a sloppy kiss and an enthusiastic, lispy "szia," Hungarian slang for "hi."

The boys retreated a bit and stared at us with a mixture of curiosity and shyness. We walked over to greet the twins, whose cribs were side by side. Their eyes seemed to warm as we stroked their heads and talked to them softly.

We were told it was OK to give the children very small gifts, so Kim gave Adam and Ava each a Beanie Baby, while I gave Kris and Willie each a super ball.

Both boys began tossing their balls at me, so we had a wild game of catch as the balls careened off everything in the room.

It was odd playing with the children in that fishbowl, with literally a dozen staff members watching every interaction through the windows. (Because no one had ever adopted four children at once, we found staff members were rolling by just to get a glimpse of us. Kim at one point mumbled she felt like we were "on display at the zoo," but we also found their interest in us very touching.)

At one point, after tiring of catch, I found myself with Kris and Willie on my lap and caught Kim's eye as she held Ava and Adam on hers. I mouthed, "wow" to her and she grinned and nodded back.

Despite all of the warnings, we had found the children affectionate and delightful. I kept thinking there had to be a catch.

Kris was the most hesitant of the four, but we had expected that because of his lifetime in institutional care. But he seemed to relish any small interaction, such as helping tie his shoes or tucking in his shirt. He knew how to do that already, but it was new for him to have someone willing to help. His caution was understandable. We tried to put ourselves in his place ... he had to be wondering, "Who *are* these people who don't even speak my language?" He was as tall and skinny as in his photo. He seemed alert to everything going on around him, looking out of the corner of his eyes.

Willie, in contrast to his blond brother, was husky and brown-haired. He quickly warmed to both of us. By the end of a half-hour, he was sitting on our laps and kissing our cheeks over and over, a stunning ball of energy. He wasn't talking much, but his flashing dark eyes reminded me of a caged animal; he clearly wanted out.

The twins enjoyed being held and stroked, which didn't happen at lot in the orphanage, to be sure. Adam was far smaller than his twin sister, fragile and shy, but with a quick smile. He was covered in what looked like chicken pox. (We later found they were insect bites.) Ava was quick with a smile, too, but didn't make a lot of eye contact with us. She was often looking out the windows or doors. We soon found out why -- she clearly was just casing the joint. It didn't take her more than an hour before she found her chance... an open door. She burst into turbo-crawl mode and headed out the door, a blur of feet and elbows.

Ava's repeated escape attempts soon became a highlight of our stay. She'd often sit quietly by the door just hoping it would open. I'd repeatedly move her away from it, worried she was going to get knocked in the head when it opened. A few minutes later I'd look over and she was there again.

It was obvious the kids were starving for personal attention yet not quite sure what to do with it when they got it. Our immediate goal became to provide that attention, but with four kids competing for it right off the bat, that became a big challenge.

After about an hour of play, the orphanage director urged us to leave to allow the children time to eat. We didn't want to go, but rather than risk offending the Hungarians on the first day, we agreed. János told us later that the first meeting is closely observed to see how the parents interact with the children and vice versa. Our meeting was a smashing success in that regard, he said, because we got down on the ground and played with the children even though we were wearing "nice" clothes. We were invited to come back after lunch, which was unusual. Typically, the first meeting is a half-hour, then an hour the following day, slowly adding time as the month-long stay progressed.

We later learned that their goal was to give us as much time as they could with the kids because we had to try to bond with four children before it was time to go home to America. Most adoptive parents only have one child to bond with in the same time period.

Clearly this was an unusual circumstance...we had no idea how unusual until our visit progressed.

We changed into normal clothes and went back at 1:30, after naptime. (Theirs, not ours, alas.) That visit also went exceptionally well. I got to spend some time with the twins, while Kim played some catch and other games with the older boys. Willie seemed entranced by Tonka trucks. Kristian was just playing with all of the toys because we were not in his normal room and they were different toys to him.

When it was snack time at 3:00, we were asked to leave and come back in the morning. However, Kristian had other ideas. He babbled in Hungarian to the caregivers and the director; our interpreter told us that Kris decided that we needed to see his room, too.

He gently took each of our hands and led us out of the room. After telling Willie and the twins that we would be back tomorrow, we crept along as this little boy padded along the endless halls, leading us silently to the other wing where his room was. It was a long way, perhaps 600 yards through three different wings, but he kept a steady yet gentle grip on our hands. Both Kim and I were trying not to cry, but the image of this tiny boy leading two strangers to see his bed was a bit much for both of us. Kris just kept his head down, padding softly along.

Photo from the first day we met our kids, Kris, Willie, Adam & Ava

Kristian and his bed

Kristian gives Kim his only piece of paper

We finally got to his room, which he shared with six other boys. He literally ran to his small, orange metal bed, about the size of a crib, and showed us three tattered stuffed animals. He lifted each one from its assigned spot on the bed and kissed each gently, then offered each one to us to kiss, too. Then he placed each one back on the cot after giving them all one last hug.

He then ran to his cubbyhole, a small wooden box that contained all of his worldly possessions. They included a plastic spoon, an empty shampoo bottle, and a small fanny pack containing a two-inch plastic bicycle. The last item, a crayon drawing on a piece of scrap computer paper, he handed to Kim and said something in Hungarian. Our interpreter said, "He wants you to keep it."

Kim and I burst into tears while Kristian returned our hugs. We really had to go then. Kristian blew kisses to us as we left him eating his snack with his roommates, who included one nearly deaf child, one mentally handicapped one and the rest healthy Roma children that no one apparently wanted.

Once outside we sat in the rental car, sobbing. It's not often a man and a woman get to say they just met their four children, but we really could. And it was just too much for two jet-lagged Hoosiers to take in.

CHAPTER 6: Making friends

Now that our initial meeting with our children was a rousing success, it was time to ease us more into their daily lives. The theory was if we hung around too much the children would feel confused about the role of their current caregivers; if we were not around enough, the children would not get used to us.

At first, the orphanage director said we could visit for an hour a day, then two hours, then more. Then we'd be able to stay and watch the kids eat their lunch. Then we could stay and watch them get ready for their naps.

Eventually we'd move into the caregiver role ourselves. We'd get to help serve their meals, put them to bed, and change their medieval cloth diapers. (Actually Kim would get to do most of that. Hungarian fathers are not deeply involved in daily care of children, and we were advised not to make an issue of it while in the facility, just to go with the flow.)

As we got to know them, the personalities of Kristian and Willie became more apparent. Though brothers, they had lived separately in the orphanage and it showed. Both were the oldest in their rooms and used to getting their way in the orphanage pecking order. Bringing them together was a recipe for conflict.

A little about names; when we got there we found the children were actually named Krisztian, Vilmos, Adam and Eva. On paper we had come to the country intending to keep the older boys' names the same and change the twins to Faith and Drew. But once we saw them, we decided to keep their given names, with a few minor adjustments for the English language. For Kristian, we simplified the spelling (in Hungarian, "sz" is one letter) but left the pronunciation alone (KRIZ-tee-*ahhn*). We thought "Vilmos" (pronounced Vil-*MOSHE*) wouldn't fly in the local elementary school, but he was being called "Vili" anyway. So since Vilmos is the Hungarian version of William, we just started calling him "Willie," and we never looked back. Adam (pronounced "Ah-*DAH*me") we left as is, but expected to start pronouncing it like the English version. In Hungary, Eva is pronounced with an "A" sound like Eva Gabor. We thought having twins named Adam and Eva was a little creepy (given the spelling of Adam and Eve) so we simply changed Eva's spelling to Ava and left the pronunciation alone.

We were told the kids did not have middle names, so we gave Kristian the name "Daniel" after Kim's dad; we gave Willie "Thomas," which is my dad's middle name. Ava's middle name, "Elaine," is in honor of my mom, and Adam got "Stephen" which is my middle name.

During our visits, Willie played a lot with toy trucks and Kristian spent a lot of time figuring out how things worked in great detail. He took special glee in repairing the toys that Willie broke, and Willie obliged him by frequently smashing them. It was becoming clear we had one linebacker and one scientist joining our family.

Even though our visits were short at first, we rapidly formed a bond with the kids. I found the older two boys were quickly starting to understand some basic English words (including "ouch" when they jumped too hard on my lap). We had learned some key phrases in Hungarian such as "you are smart," "good boy" and others, but our lousy pronunciation brought giggles from Kris and the caregivers.

We didn't have a clue how to communicate with the staff when we didn't have interpreters nearby. No one in the orphanage spoke a word of English, and we could only afford to have an interpreter for important days. Our dual-language dictionary was dog-eared by the time we left. We eventually improvised some great solutions, including using a plastic toy clock to explain to the staff when we'd return.

But by far the hardest thing we did was leave the orphanage at the end of each day. These children quickly had become *our* kids. How many parents could leave their children in rusty cots in an orphanage while they slept at a hotel every night?

We felt that way every time we left. We knew there was nothing we could do but be patient. It was just very hard to leave every night and walk past those dozens of rooms.

Some of the cots outside in courtyard

CHAPTER 7: Learning the ropes

Years ago Kimberly and I had seen a haunting story on ABC's "20/20" of Romanian orphans confined to cribs, rocking themselves to sleep.

That's what we expected to find in neighboring Hungary, but we found nothing like that, at least in this orphanage. The caregivers we saw really adored the kids; they were just overworked and overwhelmed. The setting itself was institutional to be sure, but clean and functional. The more time we spent at the orphanage, the more impressed we were with the care being offered there.

It was just heartbreaking to see children whom no one wants. I'm not sure any building would have been good enough.

We were told early on to avoid contact with the other children in the orphanage so they didn't think they also would be leaving when we left with our four. But the other children craved attention so much that it became an impossible request to follow.

Kristian liked one goodnight kiss on each cheek and one on the forehead. While lying in the dark in his rusty bed he'd hold his hair up and back to expose his forehead for the last kiss. One night, after our goodnight ritual, I got up from my knees in his dimly lit room and saw every other kid in the darkened room holding his hair off his forehead, too. Kim and I just went down the line of rusty metal beds and gave them all a kiss, trying not to drip our tears on the last one.

You couldn't help but care about the other orphans there, but you didn't want to raise their hopes either. It was a very fine line, and we danced all over it every day.

We survived by telling ourselves we were taking *four* kids out of there and that was all we could do ourselves. We were doing our part. It was a lot. But it didn't seem like enough.

We spent a lot of time learning the precise routine the kids followed in the orphanage because we'd have to keep it the same for a while once we had the kids in our care. Watching our children eat was a big lesson for us.

Kristian waiting for lunch in his room

The youngest kids in the rooms always ate first; in our room that was our twins, Adam and Ava. The caregiver would prop the baby in one arm and proceed to — I am selecting this verb carefully — **hoover** the food into their mouths. It was so efficient and quick. None of the kids needed bibs and few spilled even one drop of the gruel being shoveled in. We were amazed at the speed a baby could consume ten ounces of vegetable puree, six ounces of applesauce and tea mixed with a little sugar and honey.

(We saw a lot of tea; it's much cheaper than milk.)

Then it was the older kids' turn. The children age 2 and up carried their own glass dishes from a rolling cart to a small table and set their own place. A large bowl of "Gulyás" (goulash), the real stuff, a thin broth with vegetables, was placed in the middle. Each child used the ladle to fill his/her own bowl, and each waited until all others were served. Then they thanked the cook for the food.

To a child, they ate course by course, every drop of every item offered, cleaned their spots and removed their dishes.

There were no complaints, comments or even conversation at the table. Everyone just sat there and ate in silence, sometimes smiling as something new arrived. Kim and I sat in abject silence at the spectacle of it all. It was fascinating to watch.

Kristian was the oldest in his room and therefore the room "helper." He helped set the table, clean up and even serve the food for the others. As he ate he kept looking over to make sure we were still there as he consumed every single crumb of food he was offered.

They went potty, climbed into these odd sleeping sacks called "szacks" (like thick pillowcases with straps over the shoulders) and then hopped into small beds outside in the shade, where they napped. As we found with so many other things there, the sacks made perfect sense for practicality and efficiency; they kept the kids from kicking off their covers while they slept.

As per local custom, the children slept outside during the day unless the temperature dropped below 40 degrees Fahrenheit. (Overnight sleeping always was inside.) The children didn't seem to mind the chilly temperatures, but often were attacked by mosquitoes. We saw lots of kids covered in swollen bites.

While the little kids slept, we soon received extra time with Kristian because the staff was concerned about his transition from institutional living to a real home. We wondered if he really knew what a family was. He had lived in the orphanage nearly his whole life, with no interaction with parents or siblings. Did he know what a house is? What parents are? Did he even *want* to leave?

These were all things we wished we could have asked, but the language barrier loomed large. We wanted to reassure him that everything would be OK. We had to just hug him and hope it was enough.

Willie sleeping outside in his szack

Kim and János show the scrapbook to Kris

One good idea we had was to bring a scrapbook of various photos of our life back home (our other kids, our house, our cars, our back yard) and photos of things like airplanes and taxies. We had János explain each item to Kris so he would not be as scared.

One time when we were allowed to walk around the orphanage grounds with him, he slowly explored the grass, trees and bushes. (We weren't allowed to leave the grounds with any of the kids for a couple of weeks.) He proved to be a wonderful kid, but introverted and shy. He was slow to warm up to people but was starting to really come around after two days. Even kicking a small ball around was totally new to him. We quickly realized we were doing the right thing by taking this slowly.

We came back after the nap and spent more time with all four kids in one playroom. I bounced both older boys on my legs for hours until my knees throbbed, while Kim played more with both infants. Adam was smiling all the time, babbling and happy. Ava was more cautious but still happy. Neither cried except at naptime.

Kris played with a battery-powered pencil sharpener shaped like a gorilla for more than an hour, sharpening pencils down to stubs. Every time he got the motorized sharpener to start he'd make a joyful noise like "NUH!" Willie happily played with a coffee can full of chestnuts, one of the many odd things that passed as toys around there.

After we were told to leave for the day we spent the afternoon in downtown Debrecen looking for clothing for the kids. We had erred big-time in not packing any clothes for the kids -- we soon found out they would be given to us with absolutely nothing. In 1997, the stores were stocked infrequently, had little selection, and very high prices.

We also dropped by the county orphanage director's office and signed the final adoption papers for the children. That made them officially, irrefutably, ours pending, of course, one final court hearing the next day. We had been told that hearing was a mere formality.

The moment after we signed, the director told us "now I have something I have to tell you."

Kim and I looked at each other like "uh oh."

The director went on to tell our interpreter that, "the children have some money." Turns out, the equivalent of the Hungarian welfare system had been depositing money into bank accounts that would be given to the kids at age 18 to give them a start in life. Because we had four children, the amount was larger than normal -- about $8,000.

They didn't want to tell us of the money before we signed the papers, we think, because to them it was such a large sum of money and they didn't want us to be influenced by it

Kim and I looked at each other and simultaneously said to donate the money to the foundation for the orphanage, which uses its few donations to provide medical care, toys, and clothes for children who will never be adopted. The director actually wept when we signed the money over, which made us feel both good and sad at the same time.

We then headed for the picturesque (Hungarian for "small") village of Hajdúszoboszló (*hi-do-so-bo-slow*) where we rented a small house. We planned to take the kids there for a week or two until we could leave the country. It was a small typical Hungarian house, sort of a working-class American house circa 1950, with a small yard and within walking distance of a playground.

We met the landlord and his wife, who would be moving out to an even smaller house on the back of the property during our stay. They didn't know a lick of English but greeted us warmly and seemed to love the story of the children.

It all seemed to be falling into place.

It seemed hard to imagine in a few days we'd actually be living there with four little kids we hardly knew.

CHAPTER 8: The gatekeeper

The next morning found us in district court downtown enduring an agonizingly long hearing. Clearly our story had been passed all around the city of Debrecen, because we got stares nearly anyplace we went. City Hall was no exception. We'd come into an office and everyone would gesture with a smile and a "better-you-than-me" shrug. When someone would leave the office it would not be long before people would start sticking their heads in the door or dropping by for seemingly no reason other than to look at us.

Overall it was pretty surreal. The Hungarian court officials would jibber for about 15 minutes about something, glance at us meaningfully and then back at our interpreter. We had no idea what was going on. János would only occasionally lean over and say something like, "They are discussing your case." That's when we learned the difference between an interpreter and a translator -- we were given only the bare highlights. Both Kim and I had a bad case of the American trait of being in charge, wanting to be fully aware of our surroundings and our Constitutional Rights, none of which applied in Hungary.

Regardless of what we'd been assured, the hearing before the "public guardian" was anything but a slam-dunk. She seemed to be a very nice and well-intentioned woman, but she had a real concern about four adoptions at once. She asked very pointed and detailed questions about our desire, financial means, and apparently our sanity.

It became very frustrating to not know anything that was going on, but eventually we figured that was why we had hired a facilitator; we really didn't need to know every word that was uttered. But it took hours for us to figure that out. We finally just learned to hold hands and let János do his thing.

Whatever questions they had János apparently answered them correctly, because the hearing officer finally approved the decrees. We later found out most of the hearing was discussing our financial fitness to adopt four children.

After the hearing we were shuttled from one office to another as various county officials typed a multitude of forms, all with old manual typewriters. One finger at a time, *tap tap tap*. After each one there were a variety of rubber stamps, applied with a loud **BANG**, then on to the next office. It seemed to take forever and we never even understood the purpose of the forms. When I asked what the purpose of one form was, I was told it was to give another office permission to prepare a second form. After that I quit asking.

We ate a harried lunch and rushed to the orphanage for our 1:30 p.m. meeting with the kids only to run into our first major disappointment of the trip -- the children and their caregivers did not get the message that we could not make our normal 9 a.m. session because we had to be in court. Turns out the kids and the caregivers had left the orphanage grounds at 8:50 a.m. and walked to our hotel, expecting to be able to walk back to the orphanage with us.

Needless to say, we disappointed them and brought ourselves to tears in the process. The kids were starting to rely on us and, through no fault of our own, we let them down.

The afternoon sessions with the kids started a little chilly because of that. The two older boys were disappointed in us, but they warmed up pretty quickly.

We soon discovered that it helped to sing to them. They clearly loved it, and I am sure it never happened in the orphanage. (The caregivers were too busy and there were no radios or music.) I usually gave the kids a ride on my legs while simulating a horse, along with the theme from *Bonanza*. You know the theme, "dum tee dee dum tee dee dum tee dee dum tee dee dum DUM," etc.

Anyway, the benefit of having kids that don't speak English is you can make up your own lyrics. For *Bonanza* my version was:

THEME FROM BONANZA
(Lyrics, James Derk)

All the men from "Bonanza" are deaaaad...all
the men from Bonanza
they're all dead by now
Lorne Greene, Dan Blocker, Michael
LanDOOON....
They're all dead
they're all dead
they're all dead by now

Do tee do, do tee do, do tee do tee do

All the men from "Bonanza" are deaaaad...all
the men from Bonanza
they're all dead by now
All except for Parnell RobERTS
But he had, a really small part, and he's gone
quite bald.

(Repeat)

Thank you. Thank you very much.

I also discovered Ava and Adam also were quite fond of "The Lumberjack Song" from Monty Python and Willie loved "Little Willy" from Sweet.

That afternoon Kristian got to eat in William's room, an apparent first. Kris was such an orderly boy that it was touching to see after his meal how he went into the attached bathroom to wash his hands and after carefully doing so, could not find "his" towel on the hooks. He looked up at me with a clear look of "What can I do?" A caregiver got to him before I did and offered him a spare towel. It was quite sad that this little boy had never eaten someplace other than his room.

Kristian and Willie sharing their first lunch together

We began seeing more and more how Kristian has been affected by his life in the orphanage -- he was so orderly, cautious and reserved. Once we got through his wall he was wonderfully responsive and happy. But there was a level of trust there that we would have to earn.

We spent that afternoon playing with all four kids, until the twins went down for a nap, when we went outside with the older boys and horsed around. Kris was fascinated with how things work. On one walk outside we learned the caregivers have dubbed him "The Gatekeeper" because he methodically opened and closed the large metal gates that separate the play areas. I handed him my camera, and you'd have thought I gave him a crown of jewels. He stood there gingerly touching each button.

Willie remained a rough-and-tumble sort, and we got the impression he'd walk off a cliff just to see what would happen. He giggled a lot and just seemed like a happy kid most of the time. He had a very high pain tolerance; he'd often bump his head and walk away like nothing happened.

During our downtimes (and there weren't many) we were determined to remember everything about this place so someday we could explain to the kids where they came from.

The children were remarkably independent and well behaved. There were about 200 kids in this particular orphanage, all under 4. After that age, they are moved to an institute for older kids, where many boys are trained for the Hungarian military or manual careers. We never got a good answer on what happens to the girls.

We quickly became very impressed with a caregiver named Edit who had cared for Willie and the twins since their birth. She had gone out of her way in so many ways, from keeping detailed baby books to taking photos at her own expense (impressive considering her salary of about $100 per month.) We also found out later she had hand-sewn many of the clothes for the kids in her care.

After much thought, we decided to ask her to come to America with us for a while to serve as a bridge between the kids' new life and their old. We didn't expect her to do it; what a courageous step that would be to leave her country and live with people she didn't really know. After she said yes, many days later, she said she overcame her personal fear by thinking if she was that scared as an adult, how scared must Willie and Kristian be?

As the days progressed we were very encouraged to see Kris and Willie voluntarily holding each other's hands when we went outside for our walks. We finally started to see some signs we'd all be a family someday. It was an amazing step to me to see this kids who were strangers just days ago starting to bond like brothers.

Eventually we took Kris outside beyond the play yard where he normally spent his days. Although still inside the orphanage fence, Kris acted like he was in a foreign land. He was very tentative about going very far away from me, though he would chase a ball and laugh uproariously as he tried to catch it. But like a child who was just learning how to walk or ride a bike, he'd run off to chase the ball, only to look around and race back to me without it whenever he got too far. It was touching to see such vulnerability. I felt good that he was starting to think of me as someone who would protect him.

The twins also soon became more active, crawling around the play area. One day while Kris and William were playing at one end of the room, Adam watched with intense fascination, finally pushing himself up on his hands and feet in a crab position and rocking. He never got anywhere, but he sure looked like he was ready to go join the other boys.

Ava on the other hand, while quite a bit larger physically, seemed quite happy watching everything. Occasionally she'd grab a few rattles that caught her attention or hum a little tune. She loved to sit by the door of her room and look out of the window and scowl at anyone who tried to move her away. It became quite a game to keep Ava in the room at all. Kim would move her to the back of the play area and try to sidestep all the toys to get to the door first, only to have Ava beat her back to the door by crawling. She seemed extremely proud of herself.

They told us that one of the ways the director would consider it time for us to take the children on our own would be when the kids cried when we left for the day. In the Hungarian world that shows a bond has developed. We received a little taste of that one day when it was time to go. Willie started tearing up and kept running back to collect kisses. No matter what we said, it wasn't enough. Finally, Edit took him by the hand and promised he could wave at us from through a window. We did, but in the process, wound up with about seven other children racing to the window, waving and saying good-bye.

Again, we were thankful for the opportunity to get such a clear view into their life before our arrival, but we certainly were going to need some emotional strength to get through such moments. (That didn't even consider the 200 other kids we couldn't take home. It was just an emotional drain.)

That was the heart-rending part of being there; the interaction with the kids we had to leave behind. We were supposed to really focus on our kids, but I tried to include the others in games outside. One day I was kicking a soccer ball around, and I accidentally kicked one too high and leaves came

42

off the tree above us. You'd have thought it was raining money. The eyes of wonderment as ACTUAL LEAVES fell into their fenced world.

It was so sad yet touching at the same time. To watch kids take green leaves inside and put them under their pillows for safekeeping was almost too much to bear.

CHAPTER 9: Roosters

One day we went to the orphanage at 8:30 a.m. as planned and first went to the room shared by William and the twins.

Willie was outside his room sitting on a chair with Edit when we came down the hall. He watched us carefully from a distance for a minute and didn't move. Then, as soon as he recognized us, he let out a little yelp, jumped down and came flying down the hall at me. I kneeled down with my arms open wide, and Willie literally dived at me, nearly knocking me over.

The smile I saw on that little boy's face is a moment I hope to remember forever.

The three of us plus Edit then headed toward Kristian's room to get him. We ended up meeting him and his caregiver about halfway down another long corridor. Kristian didn't hesitate when he saw us, instead nearly duplicating with Kim what I experienced with Willie.

We walked down a long path that eventually would lead off the grounds, and Kristian paused every few feet to pick up small leaves, flowers and grass and offer them to us. At the end of the path he peered out of the gate like it was the Martian landscape.

The signs of rigid routine living were there, too. He stopped every few feet to tuck in his shirt and adjust his sleeves so they were just so. Though he enjoyed the first day, he became uncomfortable eating in Willie's room because he was used to sitting at a certain table at a certain time. When we parked the twins' stroller, Kris would straighten each wheel so they faced the same direction.

While we wished the whole adoption process would move faster, we saw in Kris the value of taking it slowly. It was easy to forget we were taking these kids away from the only life they'd ever known.

We saw this most when they finally let us take the kids out of the orphanage walls, first on walks, then on short drives. On the first walk outside the grounds, all four just stared at everything with wild-eyed disbelief. Everything was new" flowers, leaves, cars, buses, bicycles. Kris and Willie jabbered "*mi es?*" constantly, asking "what is this?"

On that first walk, Willie kept asking in Hungarian to "see the rooster." János told us what Willie was saying, but corrected him, explaining there was no rooster in the residential neighborhood surrounding the orphanage. You should have seen Willie's face when we turned one corner and there was a rooster strutting around a fenced yard.

Willie, of course, had heard the rooster crowing for his whole life but never had a chance to see it. He beamed as he watched the rooster clucking around.

Right then I think Kim and I dedicated our lives to showing our children all of life's roosters.

For us it was so hard to remember that everything was new to these kids, even the car ride to get photos taken for the their Hungarian passports and American visas.

Because our car wasn't large enough to take all of the kids, our interpreter and Edit, (we still were not allowed to take the kids unaccompanied anywhere) we decided to take the kids in pairs.

We agreed that Kim would stay in the orphanage with two of the kids while János, Edit and the other two kids and I traveled downtown to the photographer. We took the twins first.

We placed them in the car, one on Edit's lap and one on János's, and off we went. It's odd that Hungary doesn't embrace child seats. The law said as long as the kids were in the back seat "firmly held in an adult's lap" that's fine.

Willie and me on our first walk outside the gates

We finally arrived at the small photo shop, and the photographer asked János why four children needed passport photos. When he gave her a brief version of our story in Hungarian, she teared up and grasped her heart. She rattled off 45 seconds of Hungarian, which was interpreted to me as "She wishes you luck with the children."

Ava and Adam were champs through both sets of photos, two for the passport and six for the American visa. The photographer took shots of each child's profile, and I asked why. Turns out America requires a head-on and a profile photo showing "the complete right ear" of Hungarians coming to the USA. The rumor is Hungary used to lop off the right ear of anyone convicted of a serious crime, and the USA never changed the law that says anyone missing any portion of their right ear cannot get a visa. I had no idea if this was true, but I shuddered to think it was. I also pondered that a mishap at the barbershop could cost someone a chance to go to Disneyland.

When we swapped kids we realized the older boys had been in a car once before, but seeing them get in *oh so carefully* so their shoes would not touch the upholstery was something to see. They acted as if this dusty Ford was St. Patrick's Cathedral. They sat quietly, hands folded.

However, the looks on their faces when I turned on the car radio were priceless. Music is clearly something special to them, but there's no sign that they have ever heard any before. (Kristian used to sit for a long time listening to a wind-up Sesame Street infant toy close to his ear just to hear the notes.) Both sat absolutely entranced listening to this tinny Ford radio and watching everything out the window.

We parked a short distance from the studio and walked hand in hand downtown. Willie was "absorbing" the whole hustle and bustle. Kris was much harder to read, but he had a look on his face like "Hmmmmm." Turns out neither had ever seen downtown Debrecen before, much less a bus, streetcar, taxi, church or even street kiosks. We had to wonder what they think, *where they think they have been all their lives?*

The pictures went fine. Kris, our own scientist, was thrilled with all of the cables and such in the photo studio of course. The ride home was a breeze, and we played in the orphanage playroom until it was time for Kim to feed the twins. When she finished I helped feed the boys, and then we left while the twins napped.

The afternoon began with a walk. We got out the twin stroller and Kris helped unfold it. We strapped the twins in for a stroller ride and Kris and Willie spent the hour pushing them around the block with never a peep of complaint.

When we got back, I gave Kristian my car keys which kept him occupied, happily, for about an hour. When he discovered that if he pushed the key fob it lit up (to illuminate the keyhole) you'd have thought I had given him a GameBoy.

After playing for a while, we noticed neither older boy was careful enough around the babies; I just don't think it occurred to them to be appropriately gentle. We struggled to find the right words to tell them what "gentle" means. (We used the Hungarian word for "easy" from the dictionary but maybe that meant "simple" to them.) I think it may have been another case of applying American guidelines to Eastern Europe.

The following day we spent the morning going for a walk with all four and, as we guessed, the novelty of pushing the stroller soon wore off the boys. They also were having some issues listening to what we say. The issue really was they needed to start viewing us as authority figures; but their whole lives had been listening to their caregivers and now two strange people who speak bad Hungarian are trying to tell them what to do.

It came up the most as Kim and I would tell them 40 times to pick up their toys, and we'd watch the boys completely ignore us. Then Edit would walk by and say something that sounded like "tucksiz," and they would turn into toy-shelving machines. Another time Kim told Kris in Hungarian to please pick up his toys, and Kris corrected her pronunciation of a word. (It's hard to take grammar correction from a 4-year-old boy.)

Neither boy was a joy when tired or overexcited. (It was not much different than with Brandon, but at least he and I speak the same language.) These boys were so independent at such an early age that it was hard to move them in mid-stream and ask them to do something else.

We continued to see a need to gradually ease Kristian out of his neatness and his compulsivity; for example when we got out of the car, he carefully fastened all of five of the empty seatbelts behind him.

We spent many days just cooped in the orphanage playing, feeding them, and putting to bed. Kim had to do 100 percent of the cloth-diapering because she received the East-European training for this odd procedure. (Not that I minded.)

We were "allowed" to observe the baths for the children and, funny thing, we didn't learn anything new about bathing from the demonstration. I guess it was valuable to see their routine, but it got frustrating at the European pace …one day you shall *see* diapering…one day you shall *DO* diapering… etc.

It was very hard not to just "step in" and do things our way. We've both had kids already, and there's not a lot to bathing or changing a diaper once you have done it once or twice. We just didn't want to be the typical pushy Americans.

Speaking of stepping in, one day the twins got a "snack" of 10 ounces of creamed cauliflower with pureed liver in it, six ounces of fresh applesauce, and some apple juice. The boys were given creamed cabbage and overcooked beef liver. It was very weird to have been involved in raising children, including my own son, and suddenly to have two Hungarian caregivers standing over me watching which side of the plate I lay a child's spoon down on.

We do understand their point in the "training" and we had no doubt the information would prove to be invaluable when it came to easing their transition. Still, it was weird enough to make me feel amazingly silly when I couldn't cut tough beef liver with a spoon. The boys could barely chew it either, but both kept plugging away without complaint.. Luckily, they weren't forced to finish the meal.

Personally Kim and I were both exhausted, just plain running on adrenaline and caffeine. I had been fighting a bad cold, too. Getting medicine involves going to the "*pharmagynocolicalic*" which sounds vaguely painful, so I skipped it.

It got so bad one night I wrote in my journal my own headlines in case I died during the trip:

MAN DROWNS IN OWN SNOT

or

COUPLE KILLED BY SPEEDING TRABANT
Car traveling at 16 mph;
they never saw it coming

Speaking of Trabants, the cars were hilarious. I was walking downtown one day and heard (I am not making this up) a weed-whacker start up. I wondered, "why do they need a weed-whacker in a city?" when I saw a Trabant going down the street followed by a blue oily cloud. It must be a two-stroke chainsaw engine in there, I thought, as it puttered down the street.

We had been downtown (Edit, Kris, and I) to pick up some more papers of some kind, so I decided Kris needed to experience an ice cream cone.

We found a stand and I ordered three cones of vanilla and handed one to Kristian. He took one lick and said he didn't like it. But he saw me eating my double "gomb" of vanilla and tried it again at Edit's urging. Then the most amazing look appeared on his face.

He proceeded to eat this concoction with robotic precision. I mean, if you programmed a machine on how to eat an ice cream cone, you'd get Kristian. One lick here, rotate, one lick here, rotate, one lick here, rotate. When he got to the cone part he apparently thought it was not edible, rather like a container. When he saw me eat the first bite of my cone I got the same look as if I had eaten a plate.

We had lots of fun with Kristian just showing him new things that day. He loved that if you push the button on the crosswalk that eventually the cars had to stop.

I also had fun sticking it to the orphanage staffers on occasion. Every time it started to rain all of the kids were shooed inside, which I sometimes found too gloomy. One day I grabbed Kris and Willie, and we played outside in the rain, which I am sure was a first for them.

Kristian spent an hour catching raindrops rolling off the awning, while Willie scraped the wet ground with a small shovel. I snapped photos in amazement. How lucky we were to see such firsts.

Kristian & Willie playing in the rain

CHAPTER 10: You've got Mail

From: Jamesderk@aol.com
Date: Fri, 12 Sep 1997 18:04:43 -0400 (EDT)
To: wderk@mcs.net
Subject: News from Hungary

Greetings from Debrecen, Hungary, where the women are thin, the men are unemployed and meat soup has no meat in it.

That's right, Kim ordered "Meat Soup" for lunch today and received a clear broth with some carrots and noodles in it. We both laughed in unison as she spooned through it. Our interpreter, János, asked why we were laughing.

"There's no meat," I said.

"There is no meat in meat soup," he said, totally serious. She also ordered a "mixed green salad" ... she got cole slaw.

Such is life in Eastern Europe these days. This is the country that employs men to collect parking fees on the streets because men are cheaper than installing meters. This totally floored me. Any time you park your car you are accosted by a man in a vest, with whom you bargain for how long you plan to be there and how long the parking is worth to you.

An hour of parking is like 10 or 20 cents but I usually have no idea how long I am going to be gone so I usually give the guy the equal of a dollar or so, which horrifies Edit because I am grossly over-tipping. (This, however, nearly guarantees me a great parking space the next time as the guys always remember my gleaming rental car compared to all of the Trabants around..) When a normal tip is a penny or two I must seem like Bill Gates but that's not my real intention... part of it is I

53

have no idea what any of the money is worth. All of the Hungarian coins, frankly, look the same. (Using a pay phone with coins is hilarious because it depends which brand and color of phone it is whether it will take which series of coins minted in which year. It is so confusing everyone either uses a cell phone or a calling card.)

We've been back to the McDonalds here three times, mostly because it's fun to play the game show "Mickey D Roulette." You need to realize that nobody (outside of Budapest) speaks English in the service trade and the Hungarian default response to any question is "Egen" which means "Yes." So you walk up to the counter and order a "Big Mac, fries and a Coke", you get "Egen" and out comes a tray with three Apple Pies, a box of cookies and a peach shake. You literally have no idea what will come out or what it will cost. I usually just hand the girl a few bills and assume some change will be forthcoming. If she raises her eyebrow, I hand her more money. Condiments are extra....if you order fries, you pay 20 forints for every package of ketchup you want (about 5 cents.) I never did find out what a pickle costs.

The next day we spent the morning taking a walk off the grounds with the twins in the stroller and the boys pushing.

During the walk Kristian stopped no less than five times because his shirt became untucked and he needed it tucked back in before he could proceed. When you hold his hand you have to hold it in a certain manner. Both sleeves have to be a certain height on his arms. On one hand the structure in his life was kind of cute...on another it was a sad testament to a whole life in an institution where everything was so rigid. We hope to be able to help him "chill" a bit as he grows up or they will need to come up with something worse than "Type A."

(This just in...Judy Garland is singing "Meet me in St. Louis" on TV and Kim is singing along. Two questions emerge: One, how does she know the words and two, what did this strange person do with the woman I married?)

At lunch we blew off the orphanage's rule that the twins eat in a certain order (Adam then Ava) and each one of us took a twin and let them eat together. Two images emerge from this...one, the sight of the twins watching each other eat (I am certain they had never seen another kid eating before) was priceless and two, the expression on the caregiver's face when she walked in and saw a man feeding a baby was even better.

(Apparently the male role in Hungary is to smoke unfiltered cigarettes and yell at people. The fact that a man wants to feed children and even give them baths (!) is something totally nuts to them.) I had caregivers from other wings coming over just to watch me spoon gruel into a baby's mouth. It was pretty darned entertaining.

We got them all down for naps and headed to lunch with János, where the aforementioned meat soup made its appearance. We headed back at 1:45, late for our appointment because everything in Hungary is on some sort of "laid-back adjusted time." (I think it has to be a better way to live, the calm "when it happens, it happens" way of life but it is driving us slowly nuts.)

We took all four kids for another outing; this time we took them on a walk over to the hotel to show them where we are sleeping. We didn't take them up to the room because we could not navigate the stairs with the stroller (and we didn't want the kids to be frightened by the empty Coke bottles and Rice-Krispie-treat wrappers that littered our room.)

The hotel was pretty crowded because the pro basketball team representing the United Arab Emirates is staying in the rest of our tiny hotel. They are the shortest basketball team in history and are coached by a guy from Arizona. The center, who is about six feet tall, wears teddy bear slippers everywhere he goes.

Anyway, after the walk we tried to interest the boys in a soccer game but they were so interested in random pieces of wood in the grass that it was impossible to keep them focused. (Instruction is hell when everything is new.) So we picked up pieces of twigs in the grass for an hour.

We fed the twins again (kids here eat more little meals, the big one at noon) and then bid them and Willie farewell for the day to spend some one on one time with Kris. We decided to take him to the train station to show him his first train. I would have liked it to be one of France's SuperTrains, the 120 mph "TGV" for "Tres Grande Vitesse" or "Very Fast Train". Instead it was a Hungarian VOTWGITMP or "Very Old Train We Got In the Marshall Plan."

(It's amazing people trust their lives to these rolling pieces of crap, which are loaded to the gills with people, livestock and cargo. I guess they have no choice but some of them look terrifying.)

While we were waiting for János to purchase his ticket for this trip to Budapest tomorrow, I tried to interest Kris in riding a plastic pony. He'd sit on it but would not let me stick 20 Forints in it to start her up.

We spent the remaining time swinging him high in the air as we walked with one hand in each of ours. He loved that.

János then got it into his head that there was a Pizza Hut in Debrecen and we needed to find it. As we were walking downtown I heard those words that every father dreads "Pisilni kell", meaning, "I gotta pee."

Downtown Debrecen is much like Chicago in that it is built up wall to wall. Also, every store closes at 6 p.m weeknights. So I am walking in a country where every store is closed and the kid's gotta pee.

I look to János for assistance and he says (it's critical you insert a European accent when you read this) "We find a bush." Only it's not "bush" it's "booosh." So Kim and I look at each other and he says "It happens all the time. We just find a booosh." And I am thinking, one, I can't believe my child is about to pee in the middle of a European city and two, the odds of us finding a booosh here are slim.

But we turn a corner and damn if there's not a secluded booosh right there. (János seemingly knows everything.) And now I am thinking if everyone does this in Hungary, this has GOT to be Debrecen's most unhappy booosh.

So Kris with not a moment's hesitation drops trou and lets it fly. Kim happens to kill time by mentioning how unlucky it was that the stores were all closed. János mentions, "it would not matter, they don't have bathrooms anyway." Kim incredibly keeps going with this line of questioning and asks, "What if it's a little girl" and inside I am begging János not to hear the question but he opines, "They just squat."

Well this is more information than we need so after Kris is done we head back to the orphanage, which incidentally is called "Csecsemoothona" on the sign out front.

Anyway, Kim gave Kristian his bath and he had his evening meal of bread and chitlin spread , hot cocoa and tea. (Go ahead, ask what "chitlin spread" is…I did. It's a fat surrounding the large intestines of a pig. This from a country that serves bone marrow as an entree and charges 1,000 Forints for it.)

I am sorry I asked and happy I grew up in Chicago where the only pigs I knew about were being carried by Gayle Sayers in Soldier Field.

Anyway, we colored with him for a while as his roommates got ready for their bedtime and finally tucked him in for the night on his small bed. We have plans to head back there tomorrow morning as scheduled. They will have one more night here before starting the rest of their lives.

Assuming it all goes like clockwork.

More Later,

Love

Jim

CHAPTER 11: Farewell

From: Jamesderk@aol.com
Date: Thurs 18 Sep 1997 17:04:43 -0400 (EDT)
To: wderk@mcs.net
Subject: Free at last

Telling the story of this day won't be terribly easy...I can jump to the good part...we have four children in our little bungalow...two of them are sleeping with more or less full bellies and two of them are making fart noises to each other in a double bed.

Sounds successful to me.

Where to start....I guess chronologically. We got a good night's sleep for once after I spent the early evening swatting mosquitoes with one of Willie's diapers. That helped a lot as did my finally catching Brandon before he headed out to school for a quick chat. Miss him more than I can say.

We headed out early to catch the store opening at 9 to get some bibs and exchange some shoes we had bought yesterday for the twins...they had given us two different sizes in the store. We managed to pantomime the exchange. Well, Kim did actually...I am finding she has lots more patience than I in dealing with sometimes surly Eastern Europeans. I keep muttering to Kim "Don't mention the war" a la Fawlty Towers every time we run into a rude local. I also keep muttering one of János's admonitions that it is rude for a man to open a door for a woman in a restaurant because he should enter first "in case there is a bar fight."

Anyway, we made it through the store and ended up on time for our appointment at 10 with the orphanage people downtown to get the final decree.

We met our Hungarian lawyer, Eva, and our interpreter, Erica, and settled in to the office for a long wait while they processed stuff. Eventually they prepared the form asking the registrar to prepare the decree, the decree and the form asking the registrar to approve his own form.

No wonder they lost the Cold War.

(That and I am now staring at a Coke bottle emblazoned with the catchy word "Great" except in Hungarian it is spelled " Visszaváltható ".)

Anyway, we got the decree and headed up the road to another office to file it only to find the filing office is open 8:30-1:30 on Mondays, Wednesdays and Friday; 2 PM to 4 PM on Thursday and closed every time else.

Our lawyer Eva, not to be discouraged, barged in anyway and found some bureaucrat in there and basically said if they didn't accept our paperwork she was going to light the place on fire. They did and told her it would take a week to process…she threatened to go to the mayor, burgermeister or whatever they call the head dude and say this was going to delay four orphans from going to America. So it's now going to be ready in two days.

We headed to another office, also closed, where Eva also went in anyway, told our story to the clerk person who actually got a bit teary-eyed and moved our applications to the top of three very large piles of crap on her desk. She kept muttering the Hungarian word for " four" and shaking her head in amazement.

I meet them Monday back in Debrecen to get our paperwork and then apply for American visas for the children.

Because we're in the eating capital of Europe we treated Erica to a sumptuous plate from McDonald's (we were in a hurry) and made it to the orphanage with one minute to spare for the start of Kristian's going-away party. While he got cleaned up from his nap, we met with the orphanage director and gave her our written authorization to remove the children from her care and got in return a big pile of records about all of the children, including incredibly detailed health record books.

(Right now Kim is in with Kris, who is having a bit of a tough time falling asleep, holding him and singing "Lullabye and Goodnight" softly and two things pop into my mind, 1, it's probably the first time he's ever been sung to and 2, boy did I marry the right woman.)

Anyway, we headed to Kris' party, attended by most of the staffers responsible for his care, his six roommates and a few other adults. They brought in some balloons, which to the kids signal this is a big deal, and they prepared a cake…a sponge cake layered in what passes here for pudding, then some fresh fruit slices, then a gelatin. Whole deal about an inch thick…the kids loved it. Kris, always the helper, served everyone before eating his own slice with gusto.

One of his favorite caregivers made him a heart-shaped pillow that says "Love you" in English, while another brought him a toy and another a teddy bear. We gave each of the caregivers a small gift from the States and a photo of the six of us taken a few days before.

All of the children's clothing, right down to their cloth diapers, had to remain at the orphanage, so we brought out new clothes and shoes for all. Kris literally was jumping up and down when he saw he had new stuff to wear. It was touching and sad.

We had expected it to be emotional when it was time for him to leave, but we were hit with an emotional jackhammer. What we didn't expect was the depth of feeling the caregivers would have for him … they had seen him grow from an infant to this self-sufficient little boy. And as much as they were happy for him, they didn't want him to go.

It really hit us as Kris was cleaning out his 1-foot-square cubby of every single thing he's ever owned and it filled a sack they would give you at a Hallmark store. He'd spent his whole life in these two rooms, never seeing a sunset, an ocean wave or a Fudgesicle, and had nothing to show for it.

If Kris had started to cry Kim and I would have lost it completely right there, but he was so excited that his day had come that he was laughing and hugging all of the caregivers who were bawling their eyes out.

They were crying, we were crying, even the interpreter was crying, a nice touch considering our tears needed no translation.

Afterward, as I was carrying Kris down the hall to the other party, I played a game I had always played with him in the hall of humming "Baby Bumblebee" and rubbing his head in all of the plants that line the walls but after two I just couldn't go on. Kris looked into my eyes and said "La la you" which is as close to "I love you" as he can get with his accent.

We barely made it the rest of the way.

Kim and I both wanted to walk into the other party not looking like we were dying but part of us was, for the caregivers and for the other children we had to leave behind.

We made it to the corner of the hallway and Willie was in the hall waiting. Seeing us he ran about 50 feet down the hall and slammed into our open arms so hard that he busted open his lower lip. He didn't even notice.

This party mirrored the first with Willie and the twins dressed in party clothes made by their caregiver, Edit, whom we've fallen in love with by now.

Balloons were passed around and the kids laughed and banged them into the sky. The caregivers here, especially Edit, could barely contain themselves because all three had been there since birth.

It's hard to explain…the caregivers couldn't be happier that the kids were getting to leave and especially to America, which is viewed as Oz without the man behind the curtain here. But man, do they get attached.

We also passed out some gifts in this room and photos of the kids and us and promised to mail more. It was very hard for us to leave the other kids in that room as that's where we had spent the bulk of our time.

Willie and the twins also got some small toys and stuffed animals from the caregivers ---Edit gave us the toys and clothes she had made for the kids over the years and a small backpack she had sewn for him…and we tried to get out of there in one piece.

It was very, very hard for us to leave the other kids in that room as that's where we had spent the bulk of our time. We had even asked about taking home a fifth child, a 4-year-old Gypsy girl named Vivian, but were told we were pressing our luck getting four.

Gathering up the kids and walking the last time down the long, long hallways to the front door was a horrible mix of emotions...we had in our arms these adorable children (the older boys were humming, singing and yelling "szia" to all of the staff) and at the same time we were removing them from the only place they'd ever known.

I kept telling myself clearly they will be better off in America with parents that love them, warm beds and opportunities galore, but it was so hard to keep taking every step. It would have been so much easier if we could talk to them and tell them it will be OK ... but we have to know that they just find out somehow.

We ached to ask the older boys what they thought, where they think they have been their whole lives. Do they even want parents? Do they want to come to America?

The scene at the car was a nightmare...happy kids and bawling parents and caregivers. We drove away with heavy hearts.

Our interpreter Erica was still with us, thankfully, and she was able to explain that the little house was a temporary home for a few days until our long plane ride to America. Then she left on the 5:30 train to Budapest and we were alone.

The twins were cranky and did not care for our offerings of Enfamil or milk to replace their normal coffee. We fed them some fruit and are going to try Plan B tomorrow...perhaps cocoa or something else. We also need to find another crib either to buy or rent because the one we brought is too small for Ava, who sleeps like a linebacker, we now discover.

Kris and Willie have been a little rowdy but that's expected in a totally new place. Poor Kris is still looking for places to hang up his towel and still takes 10 spits before swallowing his last drop of water after brushing his teeth. But we are making small strides...he will now let us help him brush where he used to pride himself on doing it all himself. Deep down I think we have a kid here who would love not to do some things for himself.

We're looking forward to getting him home so he can be a little kid for a change.

Love,

Jim

CHAPTER 12: On our own

Our first day as full-time parents of these children was amazingly stressful. We did expect certain problems on our first day but nothing really prepared us well enough.

Taken in chronological order, Kris had some nightmares that kept him up a lot and Willie, who was bunked in the same room, really just got woken up as a by-product of Kris's troubles. I had to lay down with both boys for part of the night, but because they sleep on feather duvets and pillows, I paid for it the next day with allergies.

It was the first time either one of them had slept on a pillow, so it was kind of neat to see them snuggle into one for the first time. As a bizarre testament to their lives in the orphanage, neither kid was actually using it after a few hours. Both had twisted around in their beds so their heads faced north: the same way they used to sleep at the orphanage.

The twins basically slept through the night with some fits in the middle of the night that lasted a few minutes. Trouble is, we were running out of things to feed them. They had rejected an astonishing variety of ready-made baby foods, then lots of things Kim had lovingly cooked and even the Enfamil we brought from the States. They wouldn't drink milk but seemed to love coffee, so we reluctantly added that to the mix.

All of the kids were up by 6:20 a.m., pretty much on target with their orphanage wake-up time. Kristian threw two major tantrums before we even got them dressed. The littlest things seemed to just set him off, like if he had to pull up his pants *before* he flushed the toilet.

Adam & Ava with a towel DMZ between

Willie & Kris with a dozen varieties of baby food for the twins

We decided to head to the nearest playground to get out of the house. They had never seen one before, so we spent a lot of time coaxing them into trying a slide and swings. They seemed to like swings and teeter-totters but weren't so crazy about slides. American lawyers would have had a field day at this playground, which was made out of old trees bolted together.

Kris had another tantrum while there because he did not want to hold anyone's hand and just thought it was peachy fun to bolt across the street.

After the playground we came home for snack and naps and the twins became the holy terror this time. Nothing we could give them to eat seemed to please them. (That went double for Ava, our apparent picky eater.) Both babies took turns screaming. We eventually got the boys down for a nap. Willie was up in 90 minutes, but Kris slept twice that long. After his nap Kristian was a different child… "perfect" was the adjective that came to mind.

We took a family walk around Hajdúszoboszló for about an hour with the twins in the stroller, Kim carrying Kris on her back, and Willie helping me push. We got home, bathed the twins, and tried to feed the group warm cocoa, which seemed to be mildly accepted.

We tried to put the twins down in the play area to give the older boys their baths, but we'd created somewhat of a monster in that regard. In the orphanage these babies got little personal attention, but over the last three weeks we'd played with them and held them so much that they screamed bloody murder if we put them down even for a moment. So there wasn't a task we did in the rental house without one of us carrying at least one baby.

So with one twin screaming and me feeding the other one, Kim drew the short straw that was Willie for his bath. Well, he threw a fit that defies description. I am not kidding in the least in saying neighbors came to see what was the commotion. Willie was screaming at the top of his lungs "**NEM NEM NEM**" (no, no, no) when Kim started the water running. And it got worse from there. (Our landlords burst in without knocking thinking, I am sure, that one of us was trying to drown the child in the tub.)

What's odd is they received baths every day at the orphanage so we knew he wasn't afraid of the water. The only thing we could figure was Willie's former bathtub was small and blue and this one was large and white.

Regardless, this was a *fit*. Kim, being the everlasting trouper, actually got him sort of clean but afterwards he sat in the bathroom dripping wet, rocking himself, sucking his thumb and whimpering. We tried to comfort him, of course, but he was clearly not a happy little wet dude.

I gave Kris a bath next and I was braced for a replay but he was an angel, even trying out the handheld European shower thing for the first time. He took particular glee in spraying the walls of the bathroom and his new father.

Kim's dinner of homemade soup was a hit with the older boys (Veggies are cheap and plentiful here…I bought a head of cauliflower the size of a small basketball for about a quarter.)

After dinner I got the twins to settle down while Kim worked on the boys. Willie sucked his thumb and walked around with a small pillow from the orphanage, so he clearly felt a little out of place. We got our kisses from the boys (from Kris it's a military precision of one on each cheek, one on each eye, one on the lips and one on the forehead). Kris muttered "I la lou," and Willie tried to muster up something that sounded like "Looby doo."

Close enough for us.

Kim and I were both beyond exhausted and stressed out by this point. This would have been a good time for a large bottle of wine but because I don't drink one had to improvise. After the kids finally fell asleep I drove to a gas station on the highway and bought six Eskimo Pies, earning me some more stares. I tried to explain in my basic Hungarian that I had four children but don't think they bought the story. (Either way I did give Kim one before I ate the other five.)

The next day Edit came to visit from Debrecen, partially to say hello to the kids and partially to answer an SOS call from us because the twins had basically quit eating. I had to drive 30 minutes to Debrecen to pick her up, and while there she also helped me at the pharmacy. I needed to find some medicine for Adam's welts, caused by infected mosquito bites. The poor kid was covered with them. When he was in a hot bathtub it looked like the worst case of child abuse.

The ever-present mosquitoes also attacked us in our bedroom, so we tried to kill as many as we could find in the house before we nodded off. But it was terribly frustrating. During the day, we tried to have as few windows open as possible because of the likelihood of letting in more mosquitoes. But if we didn't open up the house, we all sweltered.

Edit, Kristian and I also stopped at the grocery store on the way back. Edit bought (of all things) "vegetable marrow" a foul-smelling, green bile concoction, and some other stuff I didn't recognize. She arrived at our charming bungalow and heated the food up on the small stove. Kim and I exchanged smug looks (sure they are going to eat this *goop*, we thought), but we watched in amazement as the twins munched the whole bowl up.

At least they started eating. And we learned to respect Edit even more.

The twins remained quite cranky, either wanting to be held or wanting to be fed all day. Carrying them all day with two other kids in this small house wasn't possible, so there was a lot of chaos. Kris had been perfect with me on the car ride to Debrecen but two hours later was melting down, big-time.

Kristian's temper tantrums and mood variations were getting harder for us to understand. The language barrier was hard to deal with in the best of situations and poor Kris is such a structured child that we wished we could have explained more to him. Kim and I had to remind ourselves that he only just turned four. He's so advanced in so many ways that sometimes it's honestly scary.

One day he noticed there was not as much hot water coming into the bathroom sink as usual. I had turned down the tap supply under the sink because he'd scalded himself twice, and there's no way to turn down the German water heater ("ve vant hotter vater steam for zee boilers!"). Lo and behold we caught him under there twice turning it back up. He didn't witness how we had done that; he just figured if the tap was colder than normal, there has to be a reason and he'd figure it out.

One night he melted down for 20 minutes, screaming and rocking himself, because I asked him to stay back from the hot stove. I thought that was a pretty reasonable request but I had to stop and think...he'd never seen his food prepared before. It had always just shown up in a cart. So we had to balance this bright child's curiosity without our desire not to harm them in the first week.

He also had a habit of simply taking things from the younger kids. They'd offer whatever it was up in mute testament to the orphanage pecking order. (Because the kids actually owned nothing, all of the toys back there were community property. If the oldest kid, in many cases Kristian, wanted a toy he usually got it.) Now in a family environment, that doesn't always work so well.

The short version is that we underestimated the language barrier with Kris. I think we would have been fine if we were dealing with an average four-year-old but this is a fearlessly bright child. I was starting to think he didn't worry about running into the street without looking because he'd already mathematically calculated and accepted the odds of being hit.

I thought parenting a kid like this could be a nice challenge, one we would be up to with a little more sleep, but having him speak another language is incredibly frustrating.

Willie appeared to us to be age three going on half that. We expected some age regression as his whole world had changed. He's understandably scared. After a couple days he started to take his bath like a champ, partially because Edit talked to him about it and partially because Kim has such a nice touch with children. Four of them pulling this crap at once was hard on me, and I confess I generally ran out of gas about 6 p.m. with the whole lot. (Plus, my personality doesn't usually lend itself to unneeded negotiation. I sort of expect when I politely ask a four-year-old to put on his shoes that it's not necessary to whip out a dual language dictionary to explain the reasoning behind footwear in general and this request in particular. That goes double when the kid corrects your Hungarian grammar.)

So some nights found me on the front porch with a large Coke while Kim managed the whole menagerie without me while I caught a second- or third wind.

Though they are only one year apart in age, there was a vast chasm in behavior between Kris and Willie. Kris acted well over six or seven in most things. He was incredibly independent and stubborn. Willie was the kind of boy who runs his head into the wall and falls down, then gets up and shakes his head and goes "*bobbbbbbababa*" and runs off. He seemed to be oblivious to pain.

One day Kris was studying intently the inner workings of a toy while Willie spend a good hour carrying stuff from one room to another on an imaginary shopping trip. Both were having a jolly good time, so I really don't expect a lot of dual activity in their lives. These are two different brands of children.

We also liked to walk in Hajdúszoboszló to look at all the odd people. This resort town is here because of its famed mineral baths, where thousands of Germans come every year to soak *en masse* in brown goo. (Walking around this town reminded me so much of Robert Klein's observation, "If you see a guy walking down the street in sandals and socks, he's going to have a foreign accent.")

We get a lot of stares walking as a group down the street, either because of the twins, who do look a lot alike, or because we have four kids. Large families are very uncommon here because of the economy. We bought the older boys packages of "Puki's," (I am not making this up) which are marketed as corn curls but taste like that stuff that Mailbox USA uses to protect packages. The kids walked around the rest of the day eating bags of them. We figured it was a nice treat and it also showed them that not everything comes in a metered dose.

Boy, are they going to like American food.

Kris also was driving us nuts with his near constant urination. It would not be so bad if he didn't have a ritual about "it", and a ritual about washing his hands afterward, and if he'd keep his hands off the hot water. We did find a local outlet for Pampers for the rest of the crew -- between Willie and the twins we kept them in business.

Edit also gave the boys a lesson in chewing gum to get ready for the plane. Gum is good for older kids to keep their ears open on takeoff and landing. Kris, of course, mastered it and was still chewing his one-quarter piece about an hour later. Willie, despite constant "don't swallow" edicts from Edit in Hungarian, took three chews and swallowed, then grinned. (I wasn't too worried about Kristian on the plane anyway because the cockpit is pressure-controlled and besides I expected he'd be handling the landing by the time we refuel in Amsterdam.)

With Willie we decided to use a drink of water because mastering gum was out of the question.

We fed the kids chocolate pudding for snack one night. It was a fair hit with Kris, but a major hit with Willie, who looked like a Jell-O advertisement when he got done. We were getting completely befuddled with Will and his somewhat odd traits too. Once he walked around the whole day in a winter hat, complete with muffs, tied on backwards, singing some nursery rhyme to himself. He loved to sort and organize things; I often would find all of the groceries lined up on the table by height.

He was obsessed with dogs in a funny way…any time he saw or heard one he got this wild-eyed look and said something like, "O ta kutya" (there's a dog) followed by something like, "Ya, da kutya" meaning, I think, "Yup, I was right, a dog!"

I had a nice image of Ava and Adam as the picture of loving brother and sister but they often brought me back to reality. I gave them each a cracker one afternoon, and Ava ate about half of hers then dropped the other half in her lap and could not find it. She then saw Adam was still holding a full cracker so she reared up on her legs and brought him down in a full body tackle and stole his cracker, leaving him screaming on the carpeted floor.

We're in for a long haul.

CHAPTER 13: Getting the hang of this

From: Jamesderk@aol.com
Date: Fri, 26 Sep 1997 18:04:43 -0400 (EDT)
To: wderk@mcs.net
Subject: Send Raid, STAT

Today was a better day, thanks in large part to us taking (my sister) Nancy's e-mailed advice to just "be" until we get back, try to survive the rest of the trip and not do so much parenting. We had our share of meltdowns and fits but all in all we're not going to bed questioning our sanity like we were last night. It was a nice reality check that we needed.

The walls of our charming bungalow/hellhole are marked with the bloody carcasses of mosquitoes killed…I've elected to leave them up to send a sign to other mosquitoes that we're serious around here and to let our landlord know they need to buy some screens. By the end of our stay here Thursday the walls should look like something from "Friday the 13th."

Poor Adam has been bitten alive…the poor kid is covered in welts. I found an all-night gas station last night (a trick, believe me) that also sold insect repellent. The bad news was the instructions were in Hungarian, so I logged on to the Web to see if any warnings had been issued for using it on infants. We appear to be okay but it sure is odd to slather a kid in insect repellent when he's lying in a crib.

There were two highlights that come to mind today, one was my idea to take off my glasses when I was diapering Ava because I wanted to smear my face in her belly and make her laugh. So picture this…she's on her back in a bad mood and I lower my face to her belly and remove my glasses. When I come back up she's laughing hysterically until she sees my face…a genuine look of absolute horror passes onto her face, her eyes get big as saucers and she lets out a scream of genuine terror. I quickly put my glasses back on to show her everything is okay and she stops screaming.

In the category of "infants use logic as well as an adult" my next idea is to look at her, remove my glasses and put them back on so she can understand they are only pieces of glass. So I wait until she is happy and take them off again. I would pay money to have a video of the face she made when she realized her father had actually REMOVED HIS EYES.

She screamed bloody hell again and the rest of the day has been her looking at me with great caution lest I do it again. I will try the same trick someday when the video camera is running. It makes perfect sense though - she always has seen me with glasses on.

Secondly we took the kids on our walk today and decided to stop by the local Heliker, a chain of grocery stores that dot nearly every mile of Hungary. (Because everyone walks or rides a bike here, the goal is to have a million neighborhood groceries, or "csemeges" walking distance because everyone has to physically carry the stuff home.) So this grocery is about the size of a small 7-11 back home if you can picture this. (And before you ask, "csemege" is pronounced "CHEM-uh-GUH")

So we walked in to buy some baby food and diapers and pork tongue or whatever. Turns out they have shopping carts and even better, they had a few of those tiny child carts that tick off everyone. Well, you have to add in this picture that it is Sunday and the store is open only from 8 a.m. to 11 a.m. and that's it. (See previous comment about the war).

*So the place is **packed**. Oh, one more detail, the carts are undoubtedly made by the same factory that makes East German cars, because the back wheels also pivot like the fronts. So the carts are impossible to control even by adults because the whole thing fishtails like a Pinto with bald tires in a snot storm.*

So Kim goes in with the twins in the double stroller, I grab a real cart and the boys look at me like, "Daddy, may I?" so I'm like, sure go for it. (I don't have my passport with me and how bad can a Hungarian prison be?) So the boys issue genuine squeals of delight and grab the little carts.

The vision of these boys basically ramming everything in the store, people included, with these carts is one we will keep for a long time. People kept looking at us with that look "Can't you control your children?" and for the first time I could honestly look back and have my face say "Nope, but you're welcome to try! **I don't even speak their language!"**

We get that a lot on walks...people will stop us and jabber in Hungarian. Kim shrugs and says "Anglo" and they nod knowingly. Kris will then jabber back in Hungarian and soon the two will be having a grand old conversation and the visitor starts to wonder, well crap, if the parents don't speak Hungarian how come the kids do? Eventually somebody asks Kris "who are these people?" and he says the Hungarian version of "Mummy and Daddy" and we leave with them thinking we're either putting them on or we're insane. The kid speaks Hungarian and you don't?

Later at home my landlady's super-friendly dog wagged over and, because both boys are nuts about dogs, I called Kris and Willie over so they could pet her. Well, despite us looking at every caged dog on all of our walks and both boys going nuts over photos of Ginger and Belle, dad misjudged that because both boys went completely, utterly ballistic. It was as if they were drowning in an ocean and I was the only buoy within 100 miles. In two seconds flat I had one boy on each shoulder **and I never bent down.**

I felt like I was wearing a boy hat.

Once the dog was back in its pen they were over there like a shot, one-inch away going "gooche gooche" but the idea of a dog actually loose is another thing entirely. The petting zoo should be a real experience someday.

So basically the day ends with me batting .750 in terrifying these kids.(It's not midnight yet, I guess, so I still could go over and scare the crap out of Adam and end the night with a perfect game.)

If you add Kim into the mix, though, we are batting 1000 because during the afternoon nap period Adam woke up and, lest he wake up Ava, we took him into our bed so I could coax him back to sleep while Kim caught some well needed winks next to us. So he's in the middle of us and the second he fell asleep Kim coughed loudly in her sleep about one inch from his right ear. He sprang up like we had plugged him in to the electrical outlet. I mean, he was one terrified baby.

The kids' schedules are so messed up now we end up with two napping and two just waking up. It's a constant go go go.

Our next mission is to hire a cab to help get us from here to the Budapest airport because the kids and our luggage won't fit in one car. János left the country a couple days ago, so we're on our own. He will get the cab arranged, I hope. We have the largest car in the rental fleet, a Ford, which seats four people. We're modifying the plan to have Kim also ride with the bags and the twins so we make sure our bags end up with us and give the twins a break from the loud and rowdy boys.

Wish us luck, with love,

Jim

CHAPTER 14: Bloody siege

Every night, when we could have used all the sleep we could muster, Kim and I were either huddled under sheets as mosquitoes tried to ram themselves into our ear sockets or up fighting them with towels like Spartacus.

The drill went like this. We'd fall asleep, then one of the twins would cry out. We'd comfort the twin and fall back asleep. A mosquito would dive for our ears, making that *sjzzhsizzzt* sound. One of us would wake up thrashing, waking up the other one. As night goes on, we canvas the whole room (which is sealed with a closed door) and kill all of the mosquitoes we can find. We fall asleep. Ten minutes later, we're dive bombed again. We clear the room, kill everything, fall back asleep. A twin cries. We huddle with twin. Fall asleep. Get dive-bombed.

One day I had to drive back to Debrecen solo to meet with our attorney and pick up some papers, and I was just thrilled to get out of the house by myself.

I arrived at the appointed time in the right county office (not a simple feat) and received, after some mild bureaucratic delays, the new birth certificates for the kids. They will start their lives in America as Hungarian citizens with American parents until we have them naturalized in a couple years. We will, not because we are ashamed of their heritage but rather because there is compulsory military service for all Hungarian males, and I doubt my new sons will want to interrupt their high school lives in America to fly to Budapest and join the Army.

I did so love the drive to Debrecen on Route 4, although the passing makes the Indy 500 look like a Sunday drive. Because the traffic on this road varies from cows to Ferraris, everyone passes everyone else, usually with only inches to spare.

This afternoon traffic was light, and I did find myself enjoying tooling down the road at 120 kph listening to Edith Piaf on the radio. There is something just *right* about that, Piaf singing *"Je ne regrette rien"* in French while you're flying down the road, passing Trabants, and seeing field after field of green. This was the world's best radio station. I don't know the call letters, but it was the number two preset on the car radio, thanks to Kristian.

That day they play Piaf, followed by Van Halen, followed by Roxette, followed by an old Queen song. It was a radio station like my old one at Glenbard West High School where, when I was a deejay, I would reach behind me and pull out a random record and put it on.

Sometimes the Hungarian DJ would get bored with a song and mid-way through just yank it off the turntable, mumble the Hungarian equivalent of "That's enough of THAT" and just play something else. There were few ads, I guess, because no one there had any money to buy anything.

Route 4 was dotted with hookers too, sort of an even more pathetic hooker than typical. They just sort of stand there at rural intersections and wait for people to pick them up. Most are just dressed normally in jeans or whatever. One day I was on this same route with Erica, who took over as our interpreter when János left, and I kept seeing all these hookers then one woman who had to be in her 70s.

"Man, that is one ugly hooker," I said.

Erica looked in the side mirror and said (insert Eastern European accent here), "She is waiting for a bus."

Guess you had to be there.

I kept seeing stickers saying "TOLNI" on shop doors, but I also saw them on the backs of Trabants and Fiats on the highway. I finally asked Erika what "Tolni" was selling, and she said it means "PUSH" in Hungarian.

So I guess owners of Trabants and Fiats have a sense of humor.

I had to send a fax to the American Embassy from the "Posta" (post office), which was an experience. There was this poor postal clerk working this tired old Toshiba fax machine. The person ahead of me had to send 10 pages, and the clerk sent each page separately, making 10 calls to the connecting fax machine. When it was my turn I pointed out the English words on the front that said "Top Feeding" meaning she could stack up to 50 pages at once and they would all be transmitted with one call. She looked at me and said (insert Eastern European accent here) "goobida goobida goobida, goobida, goobida."

She sent my three pages by making three phone calls to the receiving fax.

Kim called the fine people at the American Embassy on our 25th day in Hungary just to see how it was going with our paperwork. They acted as if they had never heard of us and were -- of course -- totally unprepared for our arrival in Budapest on Thursday. They wanted us there a day early at least and -- get this -- also wanted *local police checks done on the children*. We were not quite sure what that meant, but we considered it unlikely that Willie had ever held up a 7-11. When I used my John McEnroe line on the lady ("You cannot be serious!") she informed me that indeed she was. Another transatlantic was made call to János, who said he would take care of it.

We decided to take another road trip, partially to get them more used to the car, partially to get out of Hajdúszoboszló, and mostly to get the heck out of the house. We headed to Debrecen because we were familiar with it, and we were tired of getting lost and asking directions via a phrase book.

We stopped at a store and got some more baby bottles for the plane ride and stocked up on baby food. We walked a bit around downtown, and then headed north to a new McDonalds, which had a small outdoor playground. It was the kids' first time in a restaurant, so we wanted to see how that would go.

French fries were a big hit with both boys, mostly as a ketchup delivery system. McNuggets were pretty well received too, though BBQ sauce didn't go over well. Both downed their orange juice in like two gulps, and Kris was still thirsty, so I poured a little of my Coke into his glass. He stared at it a while then passed it back with a "Nem, kerem" (No, please). Turns out it had an ice cube in it, and he had never seen one before. Whatever it was floating in his drink, he was having none of it.

I bought both boys strawberry sundaes, which were a gooey, successful mess. Because Hungary apparently doesn't believe in plastics, the sundaes came in large, edible cone-like cups. We couldn't explain very well that they were supposed to eat their cups when they finished.

We then headed outside to the very small playland. It must have appeared totally odd to the boys, who just sort of stared at it for a while. I coaxed Kris into it, and he basically glommed on to my neck, and we went up together. It ended about two stories up in a red, twisty slide.

At the top, of course, he got terrified but I got him on my lap, and we zoomed down the slide. Because he was on my lap and my legs are quite longer than a child's, there were some drastic turns in the slide. He was terrified but was sort of grinning afterward. We did the same drill again, and then he watched a little girl do it unassisted and sort of went up halfway by himself. Willie was riding a rocking horse and didn't much care, but Kris got him in partway.

We stayed about an hour, but the twins needed a nap. Kris hit me up with the Hungarian equivalent of "one more, daddy" before we left, so up we went. At the top, he was terrified again, but I got him on my lap saying "Daddy is here" and "don't be afraid" in my awful Hungarian. He got on my lap, and we zoomed down the slide with him screaming in terror the whole way. I did mention half-way down the slide takes a turn? Well, I was off balance and my weight got on his arm and friction burned the top of his wrist.

So at the bottom he was screaming something (probably, "But Daddy, you promised not to hurt me") and I am trying to sink into the pavement. I got some salve on it quickly, but I still felt bad.

On the way home Willie went ballistic for having to wear part of the seat belt (we don't even try the shoulder belt yet) and the twins looked at him and thought , "well hell, if he gets to cry we do, too." Kim and I looked at each other in the middle of this melee with the parents' unspoken code... GET HOME NOW.

Kris was in the middle of the back seat, and I put my hand on his leg in hopes that would say "Sorry I burned the hell out of you" and he kissed my hand twice, which was a nice way of saying "That's okay, dad." I hope.

We got home and got the screaming twins asleep, then worked on the boys who were not in the mood to nap.

Kris had his nightly meltdown, again about sharing something with Willie, but came out of it after about 20 minutes. He had a hard time minding us sometimes, Kim much more than me. We thought it had something to do with the novelty of having a man around but you never know. Both boys randomly act selectively deaf ... they just simply don't respond to anything verbal sometimes regardless of language.

On the document front, Kim talked to János who talked to Eva who talked to the American Embassy and they were expecting us at 8 a.m. sharp with four kids and "two to three hours of paperwork." They agreed to waive the police check, finally, given that the oldest child was four and confined 24 hours a day to a state-run institution.

I thought that was the least the American Embassy could do for two Americans 8,000 miles from home.

János asked us on the phone if we were sure we had our INS Form 600 filled out. Kim looked again at our 3-inch thick stack of paperwork and we had filled out INS Form 600A, not Form 600.

Turned out, of course, that's a totally different form, which we didn't have. (God love the government.) Our plan was to arrive at the Embassy anyway and fill it out on the spot.

CHAPTER 15: Where did the time go?

The week that followed was a blur, literally. Lack of sleep, cranky kids and more and more mosquitoes. The kids were covered with welts from the mosquitoes despite being slathered in insect repellent in their beds. (These were *not* your ordinary mosquito bites so I imagine we were seeing some allergic reactions.)

We took many long walks and some drives. We drove back to Debrecen to have dinner with Edit and her mother. Debrecen, like much of Eastern Europe, is spotted with these huge concrete housing complexes harkening back to the Communist days. Edit and her mom live in the middle of one of these. The elevator ride should be a made-for-TV movie *"LIFT: Terror in Eastern Europe."* As it carried us to the 7th floor, Kim muttered "gee, a little slack in the chain" as you could literally feel yourself being (what is the verb I need here) *"clanked"* up one floor at a time.

I think Edit's mom just wanted to give us the once-over, and we loved her instantly. Her apartment was charming but the building again made us feel somewhat ashamed to be from the land of plenty. She presented us with a meal we'll never forget; course after course of Hungarian food prepared by her loving hand. By the end of the visit I knew we had made the right choice asking Edit to come to America, and I hoped her mom learned to trust us a little.

Our little rental house remained what it was. Kim thought it had a little charm…I disliked it a lot. Either way, we were apparently lucky to have it. My biggest struggle was not being able to phone home to talk to Brandon. When we negotiated for the place through János we insisted on having a phone, which wasn't there when we moved in. We endured a major struggle with the landlords to put one in.

I had been getting up at 2 AM to use a pay-phone about a mile away. If we were sleeping normally that would be an inconvenience. As it was, we were getting little sleep at all, so waking up at 2 really stinks.

Anyway, it was 20 degrees C outside, which translates to "frigging cold" for Midwesterners. After my phone call (depositing about five pounds of coins per call) I came back to bed on the box springs, and Kim and I both ended up shivering and dodging mosquitoes.

Finally fed up with our living conditions we pop a cork and call János, who by this time is back home in Hawaii. We tell him to help us find a new house. In desperation I even called American Express in Budapest, because they promise "Global Assist" for any problem, anywhere in the world, 24 hours a day. The 24-hour Global Assist number for Budapest rings and rings. No one answers. So I called Amex in the states, depositing five pounds of coins into the pay phone. Their "Global Assist" was to give me the number of Amex in Budapest.

I cut up the card and threw it away.

We also were without an interpreter, which made negotiations with our landlord over the phone even more difficult. (The landlord's daughter showed up with her teen-age son, who we were told spoke English. Despite his best efforts he was at the "Run Spot Run" level in English.)

After much international wrangling and many pantomimes, we finally we got the house situation at least stabilized. The landlords agreed to turn the heat on, though they thought we were out of our minds for wanting it. (Who needs heat when inside your house is 40 degrees?)

We also got a phone after I offered to give the landlord a gigantic cash deposit to ease his mind that I was not going to ring up a gigantic phone bill and skip out on him. I just didn't want to set another alarm clock for 2 AM to call my son again.

Nothing could be done about the mosquitoes.

When both older boys were well-rested they were just grand kids, but again, part of the orphanage problem is fundamental in small-group living.

When one kid is up, everybody's up and that stayed true in our rental house as the first kid out of bed usually made a hellacious noise.

It will be so interesting to see what will happen when they don't have to get up until they want to get up and there aren't clattering carts, slamming doors and raving roommates to wake them.

The twins were getting a tad easier – keep their tummies topped off and they are happy little campers. We have no idea what we will do with any of their diets. They all drink weak coffee and tea. The twins before bed have a bottle and a half of weak coffee (!) and milk. Into their crib they go and off to sleep. Ava last night was having some trouble falling asleep, and so Adam was awake too because she was rolling around. (Hmmm, I wonder if it could be the bottle and a half of *coffee* keeping them awake?)

I rubbed both of their bellies and backs and sang them a song and they were both asleep, no kidding, 40 seconds flat. It's so obvious that these kids need some affection. Kris and Willie both just throw themselves into your lap and if you move your arms away, even to rub your nose, they quickly grab your hand back and place it over their tummies. I bet both Kim and I have sat for hours now just holding one or both boys in our laps, doing nothing except letting them feel another human being against their skin.

Both little kids were now crawling like mad. Adam would chase a balloon or ball all over the place just playing his own little soccer game. If you rolled a ball to him he would roll it back then giggle wildly when it was returned.

We still had no idea how we were going to keep them occupied on our 20 hours of airline flights back home. There's no chance they will sleep, and we did not buy seats for the twins. So they will have to be on our laps the whole time.

Let's hope the airliner has a playground on it.

CHAPTER 16: Fare thee well, mosquitoes

From: Jamesderk@aol.com
Date: Mon, 30 Sep 1997 18:04:43 -0400 (EDT)
To: Mom (jedcx@aol.com)
Subject: One more day, one day more

The children are in bed and to the best of our knowledge, all are breathing. That was a pretty major accomplishment after today, our last here in eastern Hungary. Now on to Budapest!

Suffice to say the kids have destroyed our little bungalow/hellhole so cleaning up should be quite a challenge seeing as the only cleaning supplies we have are a small sponge and Willie's blanket.

We took another small road trip in the AM to downtown Hajdúszoboszló to get a few more supplies for the plane trip, which still has us terrified. I bought some small puzzles for the boys, who seem totally befuddled by the concept of puzzles. (They never had toys with small parts at the orphanage lest one piece get lost, stolen or eaten, rendering the whole toy a goner.)

All of the kids were in foul moods this morning so we cut the trip short, got everyone fed and into bed for naps, with higher hopes for the afternoon. The twins got up way too soon; first Adam then Ava, who has been in a foul mood ("Feed meeeee, hold meeeee") seemingly for the week. Part of it is we need to get them in separate cribs because they keep kicking the crap outta each other all day and night.

The boys napped for more than three hours and even slept through a visit by our attorney, Eva, who delivered all of our Hungarian documents including passports, papers and birth certificates for the kids. I've never wanted to hug someone so much in my life.

Kim also called the American Embassy again to confirm our appointment Friday at 8 a.m. and this time the Americans acted like this was the first time they had heard we were adopting four children at once (they were expecting two). Though we discussed all of this with INS officials in Indianapolis and talked to the same lady at the Embassy Monday afternoon, and all assured us it was no problem, it of course, is.

The Embassy put a group of people on our case and hoped to have it resolved in time. (Instead of being helpful to American adopting children, the INS folks overall just seem surly.) However, the American Embassy-approved doctor has agreed to come to our hotel Thursday night and do the medical exams of the children there, saving us a huge hassle. Otherwise we'd lose a day going to a hospital to find him. So that's a huge win for our side.

After spending part of the afternoon filling out Immigration forms brought by Eva, I had a renewed sense of pride in the USA and its attempts to screen the people attempting to visit our great land. Here, unedited in any way, are some of the questions to which you are supposed to answer YES or NO (after they tell you that answering NO to any question automatically denies one a visa)

DO ANY OF THE FOLLOWING CLASSES APPLY TO YOU? YES OR NO?

1. **You are an alien who has a communicable disease of public health significance, or who has a physical or mental disorder that poses or is likely to pose a threat to the safety and welfare of the alien or others**

2. **You are an alien who seeks to enter the United States of America to engage in espionage, sabotage, export control violations, overthrow of the Government of the United States of America or other unlawful activity; an alien who seeks to enter the United States of America to engage in terrorist activities; an alien who under the direction of the Nazi government of Germany or any area occupied by or allied with the Nazi government of Germany, ordered, incited,**

assisted or otherwise participated in the persecution of any person because of race, religion, national origin or political opinion; or an alien who has participated in genocide.

There are 10 more questions but I will spare you the details. What a piece of junk that somebody spent my money dreaming up. I want to meet the Mensa-belonging terrorists we've caught by this clever gambit.

We went on our normal afternoon walk to the small vegetable shop on the corner. I stayed outside with the twins in the stroller while Kim and the boys picked out the goodies for tonight's dinner. An old woman rode up on a bicycle, glared in my direction and entered the shop. Kim said once inside the old hag took one look at Kim, then to the shopkeeper and said "Anglo...spppft!", making a spitting sound at Kim, showing, I think, a surprising amount of attitude for someone with two-wheeled transportation.

I considered buying a whole watermelon and busting it in the street in her memory but I didn't want to waste the nine cents.

Anyway, we spent our last night in Hajdúszoboszló and packed up everything Thursday for the three-hour drive to Budapest. The cab driver we hired was about an hour late so we were in deep do-do because the American Embassy doctor was set to come to the hotel at 7:30 PM to examine the kids. If we missed that we'd have to miss our 8 AM appointment the following morning with the American Embassy.

So we loaded up the cars (the cab driver was supposed to bring a full-size van and arrived in a Suzuki coupe, I kid you not) and headed out of town. I had built a DMZ between the two boys in the back seat so they would not get into a fight before we even left the county. Kim was ahead of us in the rear of the taxi with the twins.

First Will, then Kris, caused us to stop for unscheduled bathroom breaks... the last of which resulted in a gas station attendant getting the largest tip in Hungarian history when I forgot to get my change from a 5,000 forint bill in my haste to get back on the road. (Each gas station island has an attendant who pumps the gas for you.)

We ended up at the Hotel Panzio Richter at about 6:45 pm so the cabbie and I rushed to McDonalds and got carryout for the boys. The doctor came early so he examined the twins while the boys ate McNuggets, warily looking at the doctor. When it was their turn we ended up with two incredible tantrums on our hands…pure, unadulterated terror on the part of both boys who were screaming in Hungarian for us not to allow the doctor to hurt them.

The doctor, who spoke fluent Hungarian and was as nice as could be, was totally befuddled by the whole thing. The exam was cursory at best…no shots or needles or anything scary. But no words on our or his part could help the boys who were panicked beyond our wildest dreams.

(All we can figure is the last doctor they saw at the orphanage administered many vaccine shots to them, which were very painful for several days. Though there were no needles to be seen, Kris went utterly ballistic even at the sight of a stethoscope. After about 20 minutes the doctor did manage to examine Kris but drastically cut his exam short. Same with Willie, who was crying as if being cut in half with a circular saw.)

Both boys, we think, are simply afraid and probably near their breaking point for change. We've uprooted them, moved now three times and still don't speak their language. They have to be wondering, "Who are these people?"

We all fell asleep an hour later only to find the hotel was about 10 yards from the railroad tracks. Kim and I just looked at each other and laughed as The City of Budapest or some such thing rolled on by, rattling the windows.

In the morning we arrived at the heavily fortified American Embassy (U.S. Marines with machine guns walking in formation 10 paces from Hungarian Army men with machine guns is a lovely way to be greeted). We flashed our American passports and were whisked to the front of the line of people waiting to get inside. We expected to be ushered into an office for our appointment… instead we passed papers back and forth via a tiny hole in a bulletproof window.

After about 15 minutes of me signing things, we waited for THREE HOURS before the final papers were ready for us to sign. (For some reason they required the children be present though they never glanced at them. If we had known the process better I would have sent Kim and the kids to a park across the street until the kids were needed.)

During that time we found Edit (who had an appointment at the Embassy same day) and got her to the front of the line and got her visa application processed by flashing my American passport.

90

When we were all done we were actually ushered behind the bulletproof doors to briefly meet the Ambassador to Hungary, whose staff made over the kids a little and wished us well. The ambassador seemed happy to see us until Willie kept picking up the memorabilia in his office and nearly broke a window with a golf ball signed by President Reagan.

They then told us to come back in three hours for the final papers.

We drove back to the Hotel Panzio to get the kids a nap. I returned to the Embassy to get our paperwork. I expected some sort of fanfare I guess… instead the packets were slid one at a time through the slot in the bulletproof plastic.

As of now they are "Legally Adopted Resident Aliens" until we get them naturalized. The boys slept for four hours, so that was a nice recharge for them. The twins are sick with colds, especially Ava, so they are not sleeping well at all.

And when babies ain't sleeping, we ain't sleeping. Both Kim and I are basically the walking dead at this point. I am fighting constant headaches and stomach woes…I would kill for a Stouffer's TV dinner about now.

The doctor gave us some medicine for the trip home to "take the edge off" the boys after he saw their performance last night. (It is a suppository so no idea if we will even attempt that.) Adam puked twice during the three-hour car ride to Budapest, so no idea how he will react to plane travel.

We met Erica, our interpreter, for one last dinner at Pizza Hut to introduce boys to some American food and to have her explain to the boys more about airplanes, including that there are bathrooms on board. (Some kids adopted from overseas were not told that and tried to "hold it" for 20 hours, we were told.)

She reported the boys told her they are excited about flying and having their own beds for the first time.

We're just thrilled to be closer to getting out of here and back to America.

CHAPTER 17: Homeward Bound

We knew the trip home would be no fun.

We had two toddlers and two infants who had never flown before. *They'd never even seen an airplane before.* We had a 20-hour trip ahead of us with a horrible routing: Budapest to Stuttgart to Atlanta to Memphis to Evansville. Plus, both Kim and I were emotionally and physically drained after long days at the orphanage and three weeks of sleeping on a box spring.

We were ready to be home.

With our plane due to depart Budapest at 10:45 A.M., we set our alarms for 6:30 and hoped for the best. Our stay at the Hotel Panzer Richter wasn't too pleasing in that it had no restaurant, no cribs and seemingly was built on the intersection of two railways. We had the twins in our room, which resulted in little sleep for us because one or the other was always kicking the hell out of the other one. But we got everything packed and headed off to fitful sleep around midnight.

Morning came very quickly, and Kim, as usual, beat me up by a good hour. (If not for her cheerful nature despite no sleep and harsh conditions, this trip would have been unbearable.)

We eventually totaled nine checked bags, four carry-ons, the portable crib and the stroller, so no way we'd fit in one car. We'd hired the same taxi driver to come at 8:15 and help get us to the airport. He arrived on time, but it took us 20 minutes to get everyone in the cars and the bags loaded. Willie went nuts as usual about the seat belt, and we were a couple of blocks away before he made me realize he had left behind his beloved green orphanage pillow in the hotel room. So Kim waited in the taxi while I circled the block, parked and went back to the room to get it.

We drove perhaps 30 minutes to the airport, turned in the rental car in exchange for an astonishing amount of American money, and lugged our two carts full of bags in the general direction of the Malev Airlines ticket counter. Not surprisingly, the counter was on the upper level, and the departure lane was on the lower level.

We waited a while for the world's smallest elevator, but it never came. So I rented two more carts on the upper level and the taxi man lugged the bags up to the new carts while I waited at the top with the twins.

Both boys balked at the sight of an escalator and refused to come upstairs. So I went down and talked to them, which didn't work. So faced with missing our flight over an escalator, I carried them back up, one under each arm, which made them none-too-happy and created quite a scene in the airport. Then the elevator spontaneously started to work.

This was a sign of the day ahead.

We waited in a long line at the Malev Airlines counter to have our passports, the kids' visas and other documentation checked. We then waited for the clerk and about nine supervisors to decide if we could check that much luggage. They finally allowed it. We then headed to Hungarian Customs. I expected a huge search after we'd spent a month in the country, but the bored clerk barely glanced at our passports before waving us through.

Then it was off to the metal detectors. Both boys threw a fit again, this time because they had to remove their backpacks and because they didn't want to walk through the metal detector. They also saw other peoples' bags swallowed by the X-ray machine and presumed, I was sure, they would never see their belongings again.

We got through that mess with some gestures and pantomimes and headed to the gate, about 100 yards away, only to find the plane was already boarding. Kim grabbed Ava and changed her diaper in the john while I changed Adam right there on my lap.

She then took Willie in to the bathroom to change him and attempt the suppository to calm him down… I could hear his screams from the waiting room. Bless her for trying, but I was then told we had "30 seconds" to board. I yelled into the women's room, and Kim rushed out with the half-clothed, screaming Willie, and we ran to the plane. She was unsuccessful with the drug but it was worth a try.

The boys amazingly agreed get on the plane but wanted to sit in nearly every seat on the way to aisle 25. Turns out, of course, our carefully reserved seats, (two and two by the window, 25 A&B and 26 A&B) were rejected by the flight attendants because there were not enough oxygen masks in the four seats for six people. They moved us several rows apart with Kim in the center of the plane. It was no big deal for the hour-long flight to Stuttgart because the plane was nearly empty, but every seat would be full from Stuttgart to Atlanta, so it would become an issue later.

Willie refused to wear the seat belt, causing a Hungarian-speaking flight attendant to come over and offer to help. She explained it to him very nicely, and he totally ignored her. (This was to be repeated a lot. By the end of the 12-hour flight she muttered to me, "I don't understand why they won't *talk* to me!") Right before take-off I just snapped it in place and told Willie to deal with it.

We settled into our seats as the jumbo jet pushed back from the gate. I hastily prepared bottles for the babies for the ascent as we rolled to the runway. I knew that babies needed to swallow something during take-off and landing to clear their ears. (Neither of the kids would use a pacifier.)

I found one bottle of baby juice in the diaper bag, so I made a bottle of grape juice for Adam. I thanked my stars we had picked up two extra bottles of apple juice at a convenience store the night before, so I used the new apple juice for Ava's bottle and passed it up to Kim. I did notice Ava's bottle was extra sticky, but in my haste did not notice much else.

Both babies gleefully sucked on the bottles until we hit 40,000 feet. Several passengers marveled at us trying to fly with four little kids and soon our adoption story spread through the cabin via the chatty flight attendants. Some passengers offered to help us during the flight; one woman even started to cry. Once I was embraced on the arm while taking Kris to the restroom.

The airline commode was the first toilet Kris had ever seen where he could reach the flusher. (Hungarian toilets had the pull chain way up high on the tank on the wall.)He flushed this one gleefully and repeatedly. He'd hit it, yell "NUH" with joy and hit it again.

I got a lot of hard looks from the flight attendants, but I figured for what we paid for the tickets my kid was entitled to flush the john a few extra times.

Eventually I got Kris settled next to me, and Adam in my lap. I looked over across the aisle and saw Kim had Willie about settled when Ava started this really cute projectile vomit thing, drenching Kim in this awful, sticky mess. Kim turned to me, a few rows back, and said *"Help!"* which probably was the understatement of the trip.

I ran up to first class, stole some wet towels from the galley and tried to clean Kim up a bit. I then took Ava to the rear of the plane intending to change her clothes into something less, um, "gooey." On the way down the long aisle I perceived Ava was somehow not done with her performance.

I quickly reached the rear galley and asked the flight attendant for a "barf bag and a towel, quick." She was counting meals in a cart and said "Sir, you'll need to wait a moment." I replied, "We don't have a moment" upon which Ava barfed all over the galley and me.

(It was sort of like the scene from *"The Exorcist"* without the priest.)

I cleaned Ava up in the coach toilet with one towel and about a thousand individually wrapped, lemon-scented towelettes. I got back to my seat eventually with my now-green daughter and took a harder look at the apple juice bottle.

In my rudimentary Hungarian I eventually found the Hungarian word for "syrup," meaning we had given eight ounces of concentrated apple syrup (basically pancake topping) to an infant on board a commercial airliner at 40,000 feet over the Atlantic Ocean.

Not the best parenting move of our adventure, to be sure.

The nice thing was Ava from then on became an effective behavior weapon for the older boys who now looked at her with a horrified fascination like she was a vomit sprinkler or something.

We got some water down her to dilute the stuff and a flight attendant brought us a banana from her own lunch, which Kim crushed into a puree.

After eating that, Ava seemed to recover, but we did notice a dramatic fall-off in the number of passengers who asked to hold her.

Kris found the flight attendant call button a few times, then discovered the overhead light button and, I kid you not, turned the light on and off for almost 800 miles.

After he got bored of that, I whipped out the airline headphones intending to get Kris interested in some music. He was terrified, primarily I soon figured out, because the headphones looked like the medical stethoscope that had so scared him the night before with the American Embassy doctor.

Over about an hour I coaxed them into my ears, Adam's and finally his. I held them next to his ear, then in one ear, then out then over. Finally he listened by holding one next to his ear and let out a glorious "NUH" when he discovered the buttons on his seat arm *actually controlled the sound.*

Kristian, the little boy from the Hungarian orphanage, finally could control a part of his own world.

I was now gravy for 2,000 miles as Kris now had 12 channels and volume and tone adjustments to make. Adam, back on my lap, refused to sleep, mostly because the kids had never been held to sleep before. He wanted to lay down flat but on the full plane we had no options. Ava eventually slept a little for Kim but Willie was a handful. (Our idea of holding the twins on our laps to save $2,000 in airline fees was a pretty major mistake.)

Other bits of the flight still make me cringe.

Changing Willie's diaper any time is something of a horror show. Changing it in an airline toilet was something from a Fellini movie. Meals came and went with neither boy much interested. Kris refused to drink anything until he finally made me realize in Hungarian "there was something in his drink." Turns out he was scared of the ice cubes again.

Ava and Adam kept crying and screaming despite my pacing up and down the all of the aisles with them until I was barely able to walk. Eventually the off-duty flight attendants (the flight is so long there were two crews on board) offered us their seats. They flew the remaining hour to Atlanta in the crew jump seats. As soon as we laid the babies down they passed out.

After 14 hours in the air we landed in Atlanta, where one of the flight attendants personally escorted us to Immigration in the sprawling airport. Again we expected waving flags and "America the Beautiful" from the INS; instead we got two hours of redundant paperwork and surly interaction with us and everyone else trying to enter the country. (If we had a close connection we would have missed our flight for sure.) Finally our heavily documented children were admitted to the United States as "registered aliens."

We then had to take a mini-train to the other terminal, which set off Kristian, who was terrified of the train. Willie seemed too tired to care. I coaxed Kristian into the train with some Skittles and off we went.

We got to the next flight to Memphis as it was boarding. It turned out to be an old DC-9, and we had both rear aisles to ourselves so we spread out. The babies passed out immediately; Willie went ballistic over the seat belt. (Dad and mom, too tired to care at this point, gave in.) On landing in Memphis, I honestly was out of juice. It was 3 a.m. our time, and I was beyond done. However, we had one more flight to go, a one-hour hop from Memphis to the small airport in Evansville. Somehow we managed to haul the kids out of the plane and, glory be, we were met at the gate by a big electric cart. (My sister Nancy had pulled a string for us, which may have saved our lives at this point.) Whizzing through the airport in the electric cart, surprisingly, was a big hit with both boys.

We got to the gate to find the Evansville flight was overbooked. (The plane was a 15-passenger turboprop so I imagine it was overbooked a lot.) I whipped out the adoption story, and the airline clerk took one look at my apple-syrup stained shirt and bugged-out eyes and promptly bumped three other people to get us on. After a quick bathroom break we headed down the steps to the gate and onto the tarmac to get on the small plane.

About 100 yards from the plane Kris finally melted down. Going onto the noisy tarmac of a major airport is bad enough. But when he saw what we were about to fly in he either shared my opinion of British aircraft or he simply was terrified of the small plane.

Exercising perhaps bad parenting, I simply picked him up under one arm, cradled Adam in the other and charged up the steps. God was again with me because once Kris figured out it was an airplane like the others he settled down. Willie was barely awake and didn't care if he was flying on a broom.

We took off with no visible response from the kids to the noisy propellers and settled in for the one-hour flight. About 40 minutes in, Kris announced to me, "kell kuckiani" which means, "I have to poop." The plane we were riding in was so small that there was no flight attendant and (*wait for it...*) no potty.

So he was holding his groin and looking at me.

I told him in my best Hungarian that there was no potty. He told me there was (I was sure recalling our discussion in the Pizza Hut the night before.). I had a brainstorm and got out one of Willie's diapers from my bag and told him to go potty in there. He just stared at me.

We were 20 minutes from home.

I went into stall mode, offering candy, gum and assorted treats, even American money at one point. Kris kept looking at me with those eyes, the ones where the kid is about to explode, and saying he has to poop. But the stalling worked, and we soon started our descent and eventually landed in the darkness of Evansville. It was 9:30 P.M. local time and 4:30 A.M. according to our Hungarian body clock.

I carried Adam and Kris into the airport and up the stairs (the escalator was out of the question) and waited for Kim and Willie and Ava at the top. We walked together toward the terminal. I started to cry, partly because we were home, partly because I was exhausted and partly because Kris was holding me so tight he was cutting off blood to my brain.

We soon saw a welcoming party, something we did not expect. In addition to a few friends and family there was a whole contingent of Kim's co-workers from GE Plastics. I blew by the party and rushed Kristian to the potty, placed him triumphantly on the toilet, only to find out it was a false alarm. (I resisted the urge to drown myself in an adjoining stall.)

Thankful for many arms now to help, we collected all but one of our bags, which showed up two days later. The clerk told me, "some guy checked nine bags and this whole plane only holds 19."

We drove home in three cars, and the boys literally scampered to their new bunk beds in our new basement. We quickly got them dressed for bed and got the twins in their new cribs. Everyone fell asleep immediately. I laid down on our bed in the next room because I could not see straight any more, forgetting completely to call my parents or anyone else to announce we had made it.

"We got them home." I said to Kim before falling asleep.

True, we were home, but our adventure was only beginning.

CHAPTER 18: Not Exactly Walton's Mountain

After finally getting our four new children home to America, we expected them to be really excited. That was pretty much an understatement.

All of them woke up the next day like it was Christmas morning. There was so much new; so much for them to see. The first change: they were all terrified of the dogs, so we kept the pets penned up.

We had a great reunion with Brandon and Coleen, who took to the kids like champs. Brandon quickly adapted to the big-brother role, but thought if he just spoke English **REALLY LOUD** the kids would understand him. (Too bad; we'd already tried that a few times in Hungary and found that volume did not make up for language differences.)

Coleen was astonished to find how much activity comes with four new kids. Her once-quiet house had become a hive of activity. And it never stopped. It would be another week or two before Edit would arrive, so the first week in America was a blur of explanations using our Hungarian dictionary and lots of pantomimes. We called our Romanian friend, Anna, to come over to brief the kids on life in America, too. She gave Kristian and Willie some pointers on safety items in the house.

So much was new to them. It was something we clearly underestimated for the older boys. Going for a ride in our van for them was like the Lunar Rover was to the Apollo astronauts. What would the world be like if you'd never seen any of it before? Drinking fountains. Swing sets. Television. Movies. Slurpees. Malls with gleaming stores. Grocery stores laden with goods. Meals that include second, third, even fourth helpings.

When we first got home we discovered the boys liked frozen pizza. They devoured the only one in the house, so I made a phone call and 30 minutes later four hot pizzas arrived at the front door courtesy of Domino's. Kristian then became convinced that if you lift this little plastic thing in your kitchen and talk into it, **pizza comes out!**

That's the lesson we've learned in our adventure. We take too much for granted in this world, and we need to stop and see things from our children's eyes. The downside was when we ran out of anything, Kristian pointed to the phone.

Our main issue at home remained the language barrier. We had vastly underestimated the problem in communicating with the older boys, who were easily frustrated that their parents didn't understand them. And we got frustrated that we sometimes couldn't communicate vital information, ranging from "don't wash your toothbrush in the toilet" to "don't ride your scooter down the stairs."

Our full-time job at this point was keeping the kids alive. Children who grow up in traditional homes learn the danger areas of life gradually. *Stoves are hot. Knives are sharp. Hot water can burn you. Look both ways.*

Not these kids, who explored their new world with careless abandon. Their old world never had hot things, sharp things or dangerous things, so they really could not be left alone for a second.

As the first Christmas season rapidly approached, Kim and I faced the unusual problem of "what do you get kids who have nothing?" We decided early on not to overdo it, but it was a hard rule to stick to. Most 3- and 4-year-olds have quite a collection of toys to fall back on; these kids didn't. Our plan to play it pretty conservative still created a pretty large stash under the tree between gifts from relatives, grandparents and aunts and uncles and friends.

The idea of Christmas wasn't new to our adopted children; their orphanage celebrated it every year, complete with a visit from "Télapó", the Hungarian Santa Claus. But the American concept of gifts was a big shock; last Christmas in the orphanage, Kris received a cookie and an orange on the big day. He also got to pet a bunny taken from room to room in a red wagon.

I wasn't a big Christmas fan until Brandon was born in 1991; I said then and still believe "Christmas is for kids." Watching a child open a gift on Christmas morning has to be one of the best experiences a parent can have.

So when they woke up Christmas morning 1997, we had no idea what to expect. When the boys rounded the corner in the living room, still clad in their footed pajamas, they yelled with joy when they saw the laden room.

Both Willie and Kris nearly knocked the Christmas tree over trying to get on their new bikes and ride. Though neither ever had a bike before, things went pretty smoothly, thanks to training wheels. Kristian merrily rode his new bicycle down the long, hardwood hall, stopping only when the drywall required it. Willie tried out his own bike — his new helmet on backwards and cocked to one side.

What touched me was they were overwhelmed by one gift. Both appeared startled there were more to come. Kris was especially verbal, looking to us and gently asking *"en?"* (mine?) with nearly every present.

Our goal was to give the children toys they could have as their own, learn to take care of and learn to share willingly. There were toys in their orphanage, but all were community property.

Unlike the Christmases of my youth, where unwrapping speed was a crucial factor, our children spent the most leisurely Christmas morning I had ever seen. Every gift was examined like it was a gleaming diamond. I looked over at Kim and wondered aloud if we'd be done for lunch.

At one point Willie simply was finished opening gifts. He'd received a toy tool kit and was busily making imaginary repairs to imaginary things and had no interest in the other gifts bearing his name.

We'd never before been in the position of having to coax a child to open more gifts. We doubt that happens a lot in America.

Ava and Adam appeared bewildered by all of the activity but immensely pleased by their new toys. Neither fussed when we delayed breakfast, a definite first.

Before long our living room was full of plastic toys of every description, clothes, bicycles, balls, trucks and a pile of trash that would horrify environmentalists.

Even so, I don't feel it was a commercial holiday for us. Yes, the children received a bunch of toys, but hopefully what they also received was a sense of joy, of anticipation, and of love. They will be staying here, forever, in a loving family. One way to convince them of that, I think, is to embrace the traditions of Christmas and tie them to the generations that came before.

Soon we hoped to be able to communicate with them well enough to explain that the true spirit of Christmas doesn't come from the mall. But until then, hugs, bicycles, basketballs and lots of love had to do.

I had to wonder if any family in the world had as much to be thankful for.

CHAPTER 19: One Year Later

Following the Christmas excitement, things did start to settle down a bit in our house. The boys began to learn English and were relatively fluent by the summer. Edit helped this process along immeasurably before she had to return to Hungary.

We even started to settle into a routine. There's nothing like having one of the kids will sneak up on you, give you a big hug and sloppy kiss and scamper off to recharge the parental batteries.

Among the best experiences we've had are meeting other couples who say the adoption experiences we shared in the local newspaper inspired them to consider adoption. Everyone who contacted us got an invite over to the house for pizza with the kids; we figured if they survived dinnertime in our home they could handle an international adoption. The letters and cards from other couples calling us an inspiration were beyond touching. One woman wrote to say her husband absolutely, positively would not even broach the subject until he read the newspaper; now they have a little girl from China in their home.

It's great to see other families being built with children from such diverse places as Russia, China, Vietnam and even Hungary. (One couple, Harold and Darla Grossman, read the stories then adopted a little girl from the exact same town, an especially blessed thing. They have become two of our best friends.)

The question we got the most often was how the children adjusted to life in America. It's hard to recap the events of the first year to bring our life into perspective; I don't know whether to start with our trip to Chicago, our trip to Los Angeles or our trip to the hospital for four surgeries for ear tubes and tonsils on the same morning.

I think it's clear all of the kids quickly loved their new lives. The orphanage behavior that we noticed early on, including their obsessive desire to stick with strict routines, was gone in a few months. I liked to think our house ran with military precision, but now it's more like "McHale's Navy" most days.

Kim and I also found our grammar returning to normal after a year of speaking like, "stove hot, touching no-no." The kids also adjusted to life in a family, though having two kids in the midst of the Terrible Twos was enough to drive any parent batty. We had our share of screaming kids, temper tantrums and fisticuffs, but that's not an adoption thing; that's a crowded family thing.

Kristian remained our little engineer; he got into computers and video games and enjoyed being the center of attention. He was a poster-child for the benefits of adopting an older child. He adjusted quickly and seemed to remember just enough about his experiences in the orphanage to be continually grateful to be here. Everyone warned us adopting an older child would be more trouble; on the contrary he's been the easiest one and the quickest to adjust.

Willie became one kind-hearted and stubborn boy who loves cars, plastic dinosaurs, trucks and other boy-things. If there's a hole in the drywall, Willie had something to do with it. His mental abilities clearly were impacted by his earlier life but he worked hard to overcome this hurdle.

Adam and Ava were both developing rapidly, with Ava in the lead. If there was a pile of kids in our living room, Ava was generally on top. Adam usually was on the sidelines watching her misdeeds, sucking his thumb and waiting for his chance. He remained very small for his age.

It doesn't help that two poodles, our 85-pound main dog, Belle, and our 15-pound backup dog, Ginger, also inhabited our home. (The arrival of the kids so freaked out our small dog that she was prescribed Prozac, I kid you not.)

Early on, though, communication with our children turned out to be harder than we expected even with the obvious language barrier. The older boys simply were not picking up our language as fast as they should have been.

We finally took the four to Dr. Thomas Logan, an ear, nose and throat specialist. He put the kids through a battery of hearing tests that they all flunked. I can't describe the sinking feeling I had with Willie sitting on my lap in a sound-testing booth, blissfully unaware of the noises being presented to test his hearing.

We found that all four had hearing loss (mostly Willie), probably from years of ear infections in the orphanage. Surgery was scheduled for all four the following week. To further prove our instability we opted to schedule all four surgeries on the same morning, back to back.

Logan and the staff of the Evansville Surgery Center got a big kick out of the "assembly line surgery," but to us it made sense to have all four kids recovering at home at once. We called in the reinforcements, including my mom and Brandon and Coleen to help out at home. That morning all four had ear tubes put in and adenoids taken out. Kris had his golf ball-sized tonsils removed, too. Dr. Logan made the necessary repairs to the ears, and said all would make a full recovery.

All four came through the surgery beautifully except I'll never forget the glares our children gave us in the recovery room. But they healed quickly and within two weeks we saw a profound improvement in their ability to hear and, most importantly, mimic the speech they heard.

We had all four attending classes at The Rehabilitation Center, an Easter Seals supported facility in Evansville, Indiana, designed to catch them up in motor skills, speech and other developmental issues. Even after the surgery, though, we noticed Willie becoming harder to reach, mostly because he was a blur of activity. His teachers noticed it too; at the Rehab Center every morning he would engage in what teacher Stan Wilm called "drive-by playing"— zooming from one activity to another.

It really wasn't until we flew the whole group across country to my father's 70th birthday party at my sister's house in Los Angeles that it hit us how bad the problem really was. Willie simply was a ball of energy, prone to outbursts and displays of frustration that staggered us.

His impulsive behavior also was getting hard to control and he was becoming a danger to himself. On one summer road trip to North Carolina he quickly grabbed our RV's hot exhaust pipe, resulting in second-degree burns; another time he bounced off the living-room couch and into a cabinet, gashing his forehead.

That time I grabbed the bleeding Willie and raced to the emergency room in the car while holding a compress on his forehead. Once there, it took three nurses and me to hold the now-sedated child onto the gurney for three tiny stitches.

Even sedated, Willie was screaming before the doctor even began his work. It took the doctor, who was chief of staff of the emergency room, the better part of an hour to complete the simple task, while my son's guttural screaming nearly cleaned out the waiting room. They finally had to put Will in some sort of "cocoon" to safely restrain him for the 45-second stitching job.

Finally finished, the sweaty doctor paused at the doorway as he walked out.

"I've treated a thousand children ... make that two-thousand," he said, snapping off his latex gloves. "THAT was the worst."

Willie was even a bundle of energy while asleep, rocking and moving to some unheard song. Late at night we'd make the rounds to tuck in the kids; when we got to Willie's bed, we often had to find him first. He could be on the bed, backwards, sideways; twice we've found him under the bed, fast asleep.

Kim and I are suckers for trying to "love our kids out" of any problem but we finally reached the conclusion we needed some help. His teachers and our pediatrician agreed he needed further evaluation. We took Willie to a series of doctors who ran a whole bunch of tests and finally determined he was autistic, possibly bipolar, with Attention Deficit Hyperactivity Disorder (ADHD). It is a severe issue, one with life-long implications, but we're working through it as a family with the help of some excellent teachers and doctors.

Some of the other children are working through lesser variants of the same issues, but we had expected some problems going in given the medical background of the parents. We just chalk it up to genetics and thank our lucky stars that the kids are here in America now where medical help is readily available. If they were still in the orphanage over there we shudder to think what the outcome would be.

We also completed the daunting paperwork to make them American citizens. Like everything else the INS touches, it was a crazily complicated procedure full of complex forms and special photographs. When we took the kids on a four-hour drive to Indianapolis for the final hearing, I had hoped for a flag-waving, patriotic ceremony my children would remember for a lifetime. Instead we waited for five hours in a room with 50 other would-be immigrants and had to talk to a rude clerk behind a bulletproof window who made fun of my penmanship on the forms.

But it meant a lot to us, even if the kids remember it as the day they got to eat a lot of Skittles and drink tepid Sprite in a hot, crowded room.

They were ours, they were American citizens and we had our family all in one place. One very busy place.

In fact, the level of activity that first year was really intense in our house. The time when we got home from work until the kids went to bed was a blur of Juicy Juice, sipper cups and hurled toys. Words can't adequately describe the chaos of those three hours. Truth be known, Kim managed most of it because her patience level is somehow bottomless. Sometimes I had to go out on the porch and take 50 deep breaths before trying to figure out who stole what from whom.

The Evansville community, which read my series of stories in the local newspaper, was amazing. We received many letters, e-mails and donations for the orphanage. Good Shepherd School in Evansville started a toy drive and mailed more than 50 boxes of toys to the Debrecen orphanage. Stockwell School mailed more than 60 boxes. It was really heart-warming to see the reception.

We would get stared at a lot in Wal-Mart when we went as a group but really, we became like any other American family today with a lot of kids.

We were weary, stressed, broke and somehow still joyous.

CHAPTER 20: You've Got Mail

It was a pretty normal October in 1999 with Halloween approaching, until I checked my e-mail.

The subject line of one e-mail read "News from Hungary," but that was the understatement of our lives.

The note was from János, our adoption facilitator, saying a sibling had been born to the four children we had adopted the year before; in fact, the child been born and arrived at the same orphanage just five days after we had left Hungary with our quartet.

The short message closed with a simple question: ***Do you want him, too?***

Well, what kind of question was that? Of course we wanted to bring him home. But our lives were already more than full caring for our newly adopted children and Brandon and Coleen. Would bringing another child into our lives -- making a total of seven -- be fair to them all?

Truth be told, Kim and I already were stretched pretty thin. Both of us had to keep working more than full-time to start paying off the bills from the infertility treatments and the first adoption adventure, and we already felt guilty and stressed about the time we had to spend away from our children.

We often fell into bed exhausted after an evening of laundry, dishes and house cleaning; we hadn't used a babysitter in months.

On the other hand, our troubles paled in comparison to a little boy living in an orphanage in Eastern Europe. How could we leave him there? Of course we wanted to bring him home.

The next day we gathered the kids together for a family meeting and told them about the little boy so far away and asked what they thought we should do.

"There's always room for one more!" said Brandon, speaking for the group.

We hugged the kids and made some phone calls, hoping to get this new little guy home by Christmas, a couple of months away.

Little did we know that the U.S. Immigration and Naturalization Service would make us undertake the whole adoption clearance process over again, starting with fingerprints, an update to our home study, and new certified copies of our birth certificates, marriage license, health records and, seemingly, Sister Charlotte's detailed reports of my activities in the third grade.

We appealed over and over but the INS didn't care about us or a little boy in an orphanage. Nothing was going to speed up this process. We even got a couple of Congressmen personally involved; they got nowhere. The American red tape took more than six months to sort out. Not only would we not get him home by Christmas, but we'd be lucky to make July 4.

We also faced the huge problem of Hungary's adoption residency requirement, which requires staying at least a month in the country to complete an adoption. We not only had to find a way to keep our jobs (again) but what would we do with our six other kids while we were gone?

We clearly had two choices: go to Hungary and stay a month away from the kids or take them back with us and stay there as a family. The latter option was pretty much out of the question; not only was it stupid financially to fly everyone across the world again but yanking the kids out of school was clearly not in their best interest considering all of the catching up they had to do.

So I wrote an impassioned letter to the head of the Hungarian orphanage system asking for a waiver of the residency requirement given our prior experience in the country and with the adoption system there. It was one thing, I argued, for a new parent to stay in the country for a month, but we already were Hungarian system veterans. Surely we could get by with a week and get back home with our other kids? Surely family reunification would trump a stupid rule?

The Hungarians said a polite "nem" (no) to my request, so we were back to staying a month or not getting the little boy home at all.

We then came up with "Plan C," using a loophole in the Hungarian law that János came up with. It did not mention that BOTH parents had to stay in the country, but only that there be parental contact the whole time. So under this plan, Kim and I would fly over there together and meet our new son. She'd sign the needed paperwork and come home in a couple of days; the baby and I would stay in the country alone for as long as it took to get us out of there.

After finally overcoming the INS hurdles, Kim and I finally left for Budapest in late April. Our new son had lived in the orphanage for another six months, thanks to American red tape.

Complicating matters further was the then-raging war in Yugoslavia. Hungary is just next-door and was the closest NATO country and U.S.-ally to the conflict. The State Department wasn't keen on Americans traveling to the region, so we hoped to use the war as an excuse to get in and out in a hurry.

One of the first photos of our new son we were e-mailed

Here's part of the diary I kept of our adventure:

April 28, 1999 – Kim and I are at 36,000 feet above the Atlantic Ocean, about halfway though our New York-to-Budapest leg of the journey. Saying goodbye to the kids was tough; Kris and Willie sort of understand what we're doing but it will be hard on them to be without us, and vice versa. We're grateful that Kim's parents came from Cincinnati to take care of them until Kim can get home.

Our first problem came up when the ASA Airlines clerk in Evansville mistakenly thought he could not check our bags through to Budapest and instead routed them only to New York. We left the plane in New York to round up our four bags and recheck them only to find one on the carousel. Turns out the plane we took leaving Evansville was too small to hold all of the passengers' bags; so, they simply didn't put all of them on the plane.

The trouble was, the bags had JFK airport tags on them and wouldn't be routed to Budapest unless someone physically removed them from the carousel and retagged them for a later flight. A friendly clerk at the Delta counter in New York promised to do just that, but we worried how the bags would ever get to Budapest, let alone to Debrecen, the little city we were going to in Hungary, which is three hours away by car.

Anyway, we rushed to the Malev Airlines counter in JFK to board our international flight to find a clerk thoroughly confused as to why I was carrying a stroller without a child anywhere in sight.

We finally boarded the brand-new Boeing 767, with the signage in Hungarian. The flight is so long that we were "treated" to lots of TV and movies. The first feature was "The Man in the Iron Mask" (news flash: Leonardo DiCaprio isn't talented in Hungarian, either.) From what I could tell, he lived at the end of the film, which was a darn shame.

Now I am watching a documentary on how Hungary is "catching up to the Czech Republic" in economic growth (insert your own joke here.)

Our arrival in Budapest was uneventful but we're running late so we split up. Kim is met at Customs by our interpreter, Erika, who whisks her off to the American Embassy downtown to sign papers. That leaves me at the car rental counter. (Try saying, "I'd like to waive the collision damage waiver" in Hungarian, I dare you.)

I somehow get the car and drive to the appointed meeting spot and fall asleep behind the wheel. About two hours later, Kim and Erika show back up and we head down Route 4 to Debrecen in the rental car. The highway is again dotted with hookers, cows and hitchhikers just like 18 months ago, but we make the three-hour drive in near-record time.

We find the orphanage not surprisingly just where we'd left it the last time, on the edge of Debrecen's great forest at the end of a deeply rutted dirt road. The most prominent addition to the place is an incubator just inside the door. A large poster nearby asks women not to toss unwanted babies into trash cans or onto the side of the road, but instead to place them anonymously in the incubator instead, no questions asked.

It is just one sign of many of the depressed state of the economy here. Kim and I just stood there and stared at the empty incubator with tears welling in our eyes.

The incubator for abandoned babies

We finally get through the doors and meet the orphanage director and the staff members, again amid hugs and tears. They eagerly thumbed through a photo album we'd brought of photos of the kids back home, prompting more tears from the staff. We had almost forgotten how far our children had come since their dreary lives here.

Our newest son, like Willie and the twins, had been here since birth. The parents had been given 12 months to change their mind about abandoning him; once that timeline had expired the government had contacted us under a Hungarian law designed to unite families. (Basically, we had first right of refusal for any child born of the same parents.)

His given name was Ferenc, which means "Frank" in Hungarian. Unfortunately that meant his nickname was "Feri" which we were pretty sure would not fly well in an elementary school in Indiana. However, he already knew his name so we decided to use the rhyming trick we had used with William (changing his given nickname of "Vili" to "Willie"). That left us with Harry, Larry, Cary, Gary, Perry and Barry. We settled on Cary, like Cary Grant, and kept Ferenc for his middle name.

We were anxious to meet him, so we headed down the familiar antiseptic halls again, making our way to his room. (It's hard to explain how it feels walking into the orphanage again; I felt sick to my stomach. It seemed inconceivable that we have more to do here.)

As we walked the long halls again, it was impossible to avoid the stares of dozens of little kids pressed up against the glass windows as we passed.

We offer "szias" (hi!) to as many kids as we can before stopping outside Cary's room.

Turns out he is living just three doors down from where Adam, Ava and Willie had lived their whole lives, on the end of one of the long halls. We open the door and there is our son Kristian standing in the middle of the room, wearing overalls. (OK, it isn't Kristian but an exact replica of him, just 60 percent smaller.) Kim gasps, "Oh my God," which pretty much summed it up. Cary even had the same facial features and gestures. It was eerie.

Unlike our other kids, who ran over to greet us, he is very shy and tentative toward us, clinging to his caregiver, Katalin. We get down on our knees and play with him a bit from a gentle distance, just overwhelmed with how much he resembles the other kids. He sticks his tongue out when he concentrates and peers up from beneath his eyelids just like Kristian.

Kim tries to coax Cary to come near

He doesn't come anywhere near us but we figure maybe he's just scared. The greeting from Cary was a stark difference to the one we had from the other kids and we were pretty puzzled about that.

After 30 minutes we are told to say goodbye, so we hug and kiss him goodbye and head to the hotel a block away, the same one where we stayed in 1997.

The waiter brought us six Cokes as soon as I sat down in the dining room, proving that they do not get many American visitors. It turns out all of the staffers at this small Inn remember us too, and simply cannot believe we are back for another child.

As we fall into the hard bed after 35 hours on our feet, I'm not sure we believe it either.

CHAPTER 21: Here we go again

We spent the next morning in town meeting with Hungarian adoption officials, getting dozens of documents signed. We had asked for an expedited hearing so Kim could get back to the United States and care for our other kids.

The meetings were not the slam-dunk we thought they would be.

Turns out foreign adoptions have fallen into some disrepute in Hungary after, incredibly, two American couples last year actually *returned* a child they adopted from Hungary because the boys were having behavior problems. (You read that correctly... two sets of "parents" actually brought little boys back to the orphanage and dropped them off.) The boys were naturalized American citizens by then, so Hungarian officials were faced with the daunting problem of an American child dropped off at the door of a Hungarian orphanage.

We found ourselves assuring the officials in Hungary, through Erika, that we had no plans to return our children like an ill-fitting sweater from Target. We weren't at all prepared to have to argue that all Americans weren't selfish morons, but I guess they eventually believed us. It certainly helped that we had already taken four kids home.

There was a lot of swirl about adoption in Eastern Europe anyway; some Hungarians were upset that their children were going to foreigners, but they were unable or unwilling to step forward and adopt them themselves. (That goes triple for so-called "Gypsy" children, who stand no chance of adoption in Eastern Europe because of profound discrimination the likes of which were last seen in Alabama in 1961.)

The whole thing was more than a little infuriating, but we did see signs that at least the Hungarian officials were starting to understand that other countries want to help. All they have to do is let that assistance in.

The orphanage system director told us of a recent meeting she had with a young man who had lived in Hungarian orphanages his whole life. When he turned 18 and was released from the system, he had come to her office to politely and simply ask why they never found him a home. He saw some boys and girls leaving periodically and wanted to know what was so wrong with him that no one wanted him.

She told him that they did try to find him a home, but many people were looking to adopt newborns and Hungarians were not very good at getting foreigners to come into the country under the former Soviet occupation, which only ended 10 years ago. By then he was "too old" for adoption in the eyes of many, who are focused on adopting newborns. So he spent his whole childhood in one or two rooms.

He just wanted to know why. And she had no good answer for that simple question.

It was truly a sad story. Kim was holding my hand so hard I thought my typing days were over. But it made us feel somewhat better that we managed to get four (going on five) kids out of there. But clearly something needs to be done to get the tens of thousands of children out of Hungary's system and into loving homes, regardless of nationality of the potential parents.

Then if you take a step back and think not just of Hungary, but Romania and Yugoslavia and the Ukraine and everywhere else there are bulging orphanages… it's just too sad for words.

We told every official we could that one way to get more American families to adopt would be to drop the month-long residency requirement. Our comments were met with politeness but such decisions are made at the highest levels of government and way above these officials in Hajdu-Bihar county.

We eventually got everything signed and applied for. The next hurdle remained the American Embassy, which seemingly has to type the Declaration of Independence on every application they approve. We edged our way through the crowd in front of the Embassy and filed what papers we could.

After that we drove to the orphanage and spent several hours with Cary and continued to be awed by the familial resemblance. It was just plain scary. He'd do something and Kim and I would name the other child of ours who did the same thing. He was becoming more comfortable around us, but we plainly had to build a little trust. He'd venture toward us a little then dash back to Katalin for reassurance.

He really enjoyed being in the private playroom, where they take new parents and kids to play in new surroundings. All of the toys were new to him, so we spent a lot of time playing with everything he found, including many of the same toys we'd played with 18 months ago with the other kids.

He was very reluctant to let Kim or I do much more than touch him a few times before scooting off.

We also met with one of Kristian's former caregivers and showed her some photos of him. She was surprised to see how he had grown. (Amazing what three good meals a day can do to a child!) One friend Kristian's age, Johnny, who is nearly blind, was still there. He remembered Kris and asked about him. He stared at the photos from about an inch away, rubbing Kristian's face with recognition. It was very sad.

Some children do leave there, but they just rotate in more to replace them. In the room next door to Cary's there were nine children, only one of whom is legally "adoptable," which means he has all of his paperwork completed. One child in that room weighed just 11 pounds. He's 18 months old, and doctors were debating whether to expend the energy (and I am guessing the money) to operate on his heart. It is just sad considering that couples stand ready to adopt nearly anyone that the country will simply release.

After watching Cary's bath, we got to rub some lotion on him and watch him get dressed and eat. His caregiver set some sort of eating record. Kati feeds Cary like a ShopVac in reverse. No kidding, the poor kid ate a healthy bowl of potato mush, then a large bowl of applesauce -- for a snack.

Kati wondered out loud why he did not want his tea; I wanted to say, "Because he's full of mush," but I did not know the Hungarian word for "mush." Getting up from the table he looked like Buddha.

After hugs and kisses (which he was not crazy about receiving) we were dismissed for the night, but it sure was hard leaving him there. He had become our son the first moment we saw him, and we desperately wanted to take him home.

We drove to a new Western pub in Debrecen for dinner. The highlight of the night was the live band playing American hits phonetically ("I find my thrill, on Boo-Berry Bill") culminating with a rendition of "YMCA," the Hungarian version ("That's why I play at the OOOE, EM, SAY, OEA.") It was kind of expensive, but we wanted one last nice meal before Kim headed home and I was stuck eating only stuff I can read on a menu, which is "Szonka" (ham) and Coke.

It was amazing how far Hungary and Debrecen had come in just 18 months. Already there were many new stores, a shopping mall and even a Wal-Mart-like store open in this small city. I wasn't sure it was progress, but it was much easier to buy things there now.

CHAPTER 22: Mom goes home

From: Jamesderk@aol.com
Date: 1 May 1999 18:04:43 -0400 (EDT)
To: Mom (jedcx@aol.com)
Subject: Kim is enroute

Today was tough because Kim had to say goodbye to Cary to head back to Evansville to care for our other children. We've been making very slow progress in gaining Cary's trust during our orphanage visits. He has always been very shy around strangers and we're clearly dealing with overcoming that.

He let both of us pick him up a few times today without screaming bloody murder, so that's a start. He is starting to interact with us; when we arrived at the orphanage after breakfast he did smile broadly and appeared happy to see us.

This morning we took another walk outside the orphanage building, but not yet outside its tall, iron fence. Cary was very curious about little things, as his siblings were; he often stopped to pick up rocks, flowers and bits of debris. He showed his strong stubbornness more than once; when he wants something he can't have, he digs in his heels and puts up a fight.

He developed a nasty croupy cough overnight; we asked about getting him to see a doctor or nurse, but today is May Day in Europe, which means hardly anyone is at work. That leaves the orphanage short-staffed and there are no medical people around for a few days.

After our walk, we watched Kati feed him lunch. Actually, he's feeding himself pretty successfully, even using the same real china and glasses our other kids used. It remains so strange to see such a tiny kid using real dishes.

Cary really hates the weak tea that the kids all drink here. The kids sometimes get juice, but never milk from what I can tell. He likes his bath time but really hates having his diaper changed and his hair washed. Nearly the same tastes as Adam; nearly the same cry, too. It's very eerie to hear the same sounds coming out of a kid who has never met his brothers or sister.

Once Kim leaves it will be interesting to see how fast he warms to me and how much the Hungarians will allow me to do for him while here. My attempts to change diapers or feed kids last time I was here nearly prompted an international incident because Hungarian men are not typically Mr. Moms.

Visiting the orphanage each day is getting harder and harder, seeing all of these kids with such bleak chances. On this trip our goal was to bring all the children here at least one toy of their own. Our friend Lisa Hunt gave us 150 rattles to give out as a start. I passed most of them out today and was politely mobbed. Kim yelled, "You look like the Pied Piper" as a gaggle of kids with rattles followed me around the outside courtyard.

To see the expressions on the kids' faces was heart-rending; one little Gypsy girl took a rattle from me, looked it over and shook it. She then carefully handed it back. When her caregiver told her in Hungarian that she could keep it, she pressed it to her chest and walked off, like it was a precious jewel.

For the next hour, the courtyard outside was awash with the sounds of rattles. But it made me more determined to mail more toys here; the rooms are pretty pathetic when it comes to entertainment.

I also spent way too much time holding Briggi, a tiny Gypsy baby who spends most of her days lying on her back doing nothing. The look in her eyes is something I will never forget, even if I wanted to. (And most nights, I do want to.)

The farewell at the airport between Kim and I was awful… Kim didn't want to leave and I didn't want to face a month in a foreign land without her. But we both knew it was the right thing to do. She headed down the jetway in tears and I was bawling down Route 4 back to Debrecen.

It will be a long month.

CHAPTER 23: On my own

From: Jamesderk@aol.com
Date: 2 May 1999 17:04:43 -0400 (EDT)
To: Dad (wderk@mcs.net)
Subject: On my own

The next day started ominously when I was awakened from a dead sleep at 2 a.m., to find a bee stinging me on the neck. I, as the British would say, dispatched him without delay and headed to the bathroom. My allergy to bee stings made things a little ugly as I was growing a half golf-ball on my neck.

I swigged a half-bottle of children's Benadryl and went back to bed.

As you may have surmised, the only TV channel I get in the English language is the BBC World News Channel, which plays "ugly American" news 24 hours a day.

Speaking of the war, things remain a little edgy in Hungary. The Hungarians I have talked to are thrilled to be part of NATO, but not so happy about being at war with Yugoslavia, the northern portion of which is still populated with lots of Hungarian families. They seem to be willing to stick with NATO as long as it keeps the Russians out, however.

It's pretty hard for me to have deep foreign policy discussions when I know a grand total of about 50 Hungarian words.

Anyway, this was my first full day at the orphanage without Kim and the kids plain wiped me out. I am an unquestioned attraction among most of the children here, most of whom have never seen a man before. (If no one stops me

I also will come home with Vilma, a lovely little girl that has grown attached to my lower leg.)

I arrived at the orphanage at 8 AM and found Cary lying in the middle of one of the long halls having a temper tantrum. Kati was doing her best but he woke up in a foul mood and nothing was much helping that. He was clearly still sick with deep nasal congestion and a croupy cough, so I asked again for some medical attention. The doctor was eventually summoned.

There's nothing like an Eastern European physician to give the phrase "bedside manners" a whole new meaning. I finally had to leave the room when they were trying to pry Cary's mouth open with a metal bar to look at his throat.

The diagnosis was passed to me by Kati pointing to the Hungarian word for "sick" in the dictionary. After playing charades with her for a while, I determined they suspect strep throat or bronchitis but lack the test kits to be sure. And he's cutting three teeth; so, things are getting ugly all around.

Kati and I took him for his first car ride ever to get photos taken for his passport. He just stared out the window with wide eyes and babbled a few times. The photo lab lady, the same one as last time, burst into tears again when she remembered me and the other kids. She grabbed my arm and jabbered something that must have been "you're out of your mind" but in a kind way.

The photos turned out nicely, too.

After we got back to the orphanage I got to see Cary's first major-league temper tantrum. In the playroom, one of the most popular "toys" is a bucket of nuts that have fallen from trees around the orphanage. Not sure what kids are to do with these but Cary tossed one of the acorns in his mouth and looked at me. My gut feeling as a father was this was not a good idea, so I asked for it back.

He shot me a look that basically said, "You want it, pal, you come get it." So I did, prying his mouth open and retrieving it, which made him one terribly unhappy little person. (If he does this on the plane coming home, I'll be the tall guy hiding in the lav.)

He ran to his bed in the other room and screamed for 30 minutes.

By the way, two of their other toy choices, I swear to God, are empty aerosol cans and empty Tic-Tac containers. (We need to get another toy drive going.)

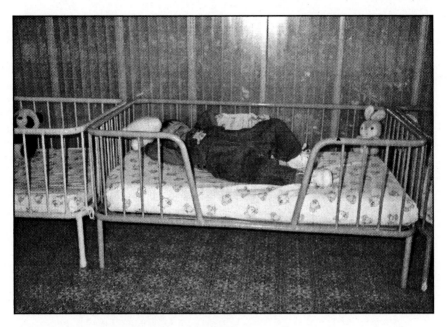

Cary pouting on his bed

After his well-needed nap, I arrived back at the orphanage at about 3 p.m. to rousing hugs and kisses from all the children except my own son, who looked at me vaguely like I had stolen his wallet.

In the courtyard I was greeted by a chorus of rattles, which made me feel much better. Cary seemed content to watch me play with the other kids while pretending not to look at me.

This one Gypsy boy, Yoshi, calls me "Bocci" (translated as "man"). His caregiver eventually told him my name, so now he calls me "Bocci Jeeeeem." He's absolutely adorable and if I can sneak him out of the country in my carry-on, he's coming home, too.

Despite the acorn incident, Cary seemed to be warming up to me slowly. I got to spend more time alone with him the next day when we walked (with Kati) to my hotel so he could check out the digs before he takes up residence later this week.

He was very inquisitive and clever with some intuitive ways. For example, he's never seen an electric cord before. I had my laptop cord on the floor unplugged at both ends. He picked up the plug end, took one look at it and walked right over to the wall and started to plug it in. (And got plenty upset when I stopped him.)

Cary discovers his left hand and his burnroot

Then it was back to the orphanage for an uneventful bath and my feeding him a god-awful lunch of some bread and liver stuff, a small snack and another nighttime snack. His favorite food is a pureed fruit that is loosely translated as "burnroot." (Tastes vaguely of lint.)

I've created some furor by letting Cary eat with his left hand; he clearly is left-handed but for some reason eating with that hand simply is not done here. We noticed that early on when his caregiver was doing the feedings he would grab the spoon with his left hand and she'd correct him and put it in his right.

Today while I was feeding him he grabbed the spoon with his left and gave me a look and waited for me to correct him. I said, "Good boy, you're smart" in Hungarian and he grinned and started to eat creamed carrots with some gusto.

His caregiver came in, looked at him, and told me in broken English that he was right-handed. I responded "apparently not" and Cary kept eating with a grin on his face.

Maybe I earned a little of his trust today.

CHAPTER 24: Banana man

From: Jamesderk@aol.com
Date: 6 May 1999 21:24:43 -0400 (EDT)
To: Mom (jedcx@aol.com)
Subject: Who can take a sunrise?

This morning I met Cary in his room and got a bored glance when I walked in, a big improvement over the outright glare of the day before. We spent the morning taking walks and playing in the playroom just trying to get him used to my face.

I made a startling discovery today, though, at lunchtime. All of the doors are kept closed to keep the kids in their rooms and old metal carts carrying food and laundry go up and down the halls all day.

Today, all seven kids in the room perked up and glanced at the door at the same time. Sure enough, they recognize the sound and timbre of their own lunch cart coming down the hall. (The same cart is used every day for the same room.)

I watched at both snack times and dinner; same thing. It makes me even more committed to what we're doing here; it was so sad that the routine is that ingrained. If you think about it there's nothing else to listen to, no music, no television, just squeaky cart wheels.

After feeding Cary and noticing the kids each had two slices of a radish for fruit for the second day in a row, I headed to the fruit market while he napped and filled the back seat of my rental car with about 200 bananas. (You should have seen the fruit seller's face when I grabbed them all. He first thought I was

131

stealing them, for sure. When I showed him the money, he kept gesturing to the pile saying "All of them?" in Hungarian.)

Yes, every last one of them. Load 'em up, buddy.

When I came in to the orphanage with the first load, you would have thought I was Santa Claus. When I kept leaving and coming back with more, I earned some large grins. (Yoshi now called me "Banan Bocci" or "Banana Man.") Bananas are considered expensive and are rarely seen in the orphanage. The cooks hugged me, which was nice.

Tomorrow I plan to hit the market again and get my name changed to "Erdu Bocci" (strawberries). At least while I'm here we can have some fun.

The caregivers here are still shocked any time I do anything, including bathe or diaper Cary. I am a man in a glass room…every time I do something domestic there are a half-dozen caregivers watching me and smiling. I know it's not because of my looks so it has to be because I am alone in a strange land with a baby.

Anyway, Cary and I spent the afternoon in my hotel room. I got "the look" from Cary for a few minutes, but he finally gave me a break and we had some pretty good playing time. At the end of one game I opened my arms wide and he hugged me and laughed, then realized he was supposed to be mad at me, so he unclenched and hid in the corner for a while.

Despite this, we're moving forward; the plan is for me to have him at the hotel most of the day tomorrow, all day Thursday and finally forever on Friday afternoon, when his farewell party will be held. I think I'll bring lots of fruit and candy, enough for the whole place, so everyone can share in the start of Cary's life.

That is, if he'll leave with me.

I sort-of talked with two of Kris's former caregivers today and they claim Kris was exactly the same way at the same age. It's hard to tell if they are right or just trying to make me feel better. It's just hard to get a such a warm welcome from all the other kids each time I come in a room and get nothing from my own son. I know he's warming up a little each day but it is very hard to be so lonely over here.

I did receive his Hungarian passport photos back today; so, I think I am set for Friday morning's meetings with all of the local officials. Once that's done, I get many of the papers approved but still have to wait for a birth certificate to be issued, then a Hungarian passport.

With that in hand, I can then go the American Embassy in Budapest and beg for a permanent resident alien visa for Cary and get his physical.

Once that is done, we're outta here.

And I miss Kim and the kids so much that day can't come soon enough.

CHAPTER 25: Finally a day of fun

From: Jamesderk@aol.com
Date: 12 May 1999 22:14:53 -0400 (EDT)
To: Mom (jedcx@aol.com)
Subject: Turning point?

A formation of U.S. fighter jets flew over Hungary today en route to Yugoslavia. One could hear them coming for miles. (Because there is no intra-country air service here, you never see planes in the sky.)

Apparently last night the Hungarian government agreed that air strikes against Yugoslavia could be launched from Hungary. Many local residents are worried about the heightened involvement and Yugoslav leader Slobodan Milošević's pledge to bomb Hungary.

*And now, the weather: it's freezing here. Something like 5 Celsius at night, which translates to **BRRRRRR**. I finally got the hotel staff to admit the heat isn't turned off, it's broken. (And they don't plan to fix it any time soon.) There no such thing as space heaters here, so not sure what is going to happen tomorrow when Cary comes to stay.*

Anyway, I got up early and headed to the orphanage where I got a nice, warm hug from little Cary before we headed over to the hotel, hand in hand, just he and I.

Hooray! Just on schedule, the kid likes me now.

It was our first time alone and we loved it. We spent the morning goofing around in the room waiting for the sun to warm the outdoors. Cary spent a full half-hour pulling nearly every item out of my suitcase, studying it closely, the tossing it over his shoulder. It's funny when he wants to do something he's not sure is allowed, he'll extend his hand over the object, then pause and look at me. If I say "Egen" or "yo" (yes and OK) then he smiles softly and goes ahead. It was fun watching him carefully examine everything from socks to stick deodorant.

We walked back and I fed him lunch back at the orphanage and strapped him into his thick, over the shoulder "szack" and placed him outside in his crib for a nap.

(It still amazes me the kids sleep outside if it is 40 degrees or warmer, rain or shine.) I kept thinking about making an issue of it but he doesn't seem to mind and it's only one more day.

While he was asleep, I headed to the store to buy 450 candy bars so each kid can have a couple during tomorrow's farewell party for Cary. (The looks I received in the store while buying a cart full of candy bars was precious, especially because I could not explain anything to the teen-age clerk.)

After the nap, I again picked up the little guy and we walked back to the hotel, hand in hand. (I can't go anywhere with him in the car alone since I do not have a car seat and need another adult in the car to hold him.)

Anyway, we walked around, played some games and watched a little TV, which he basically ignored. We also ate a huge amount of "butterkek" cookies, which do not seem to have any butter in them. We went back to the orphanage for a bath, and a small snack of a piece of bread and two slices of raw onion. (!!!)

(I really need to get back to that fruit stand.)

After snack, I played with Cary and six of his roommates in the large sleeping room for about an hour.

I got a rush from the past during my juggling exhibition when Yoshi kept saying "Maigaint" every time I stopped performing. Kristian used to say that to us (it means "do it again") when Kim and I swung him in the air when we first met him. Yoshi loved the juggling; he would bring me three things and I would do my best to juggle them; all was well for about an hour until he brought me a ball, a doll and a full-size wooden chair.

Then it was bedtime, not a good time for Cary. He cried bitterly when I left for the night; very heart-rending stuff. Bedtime in the orphanage is just plain awful, with kids longing for hugs, kisses and any kind of attention. No matter how many kids you cheer up a little bit, it's just sad that all these kids are going to bed in rusty metal beds without mommy or daddy to hug.

I never left there without sobbing.

Tomorrow, with any luck, will be his last day in this place.

CHAPTER 26: Another farewell

From: Jamesderk@aol.com
Date: 15 May 1999 23:24:53 -0400 (EDT)
To: Dad (wderk@mcs.net)
Subject: Farewell, redux

An absolute pledge: I will never, ever attend another farewell celebration at an orphanage. I think I used up my ability to cope with raw emotions when Kim and I took the other four kids home. This one was even worse.

Anyway, I am starting in the middle. I woke up early again this morning to get ready for meetings all morning with officials to sign papers. Caught enough of the BBC news to hear that searchers had discovered the frozen remains of a Brit who had attempted to climb Everest 75 years ago, about 40 years before Sir Edmund Hillary. The big question is did he die on the way down after making the summit or on the way up? Then came this:

ANNOUNCER: "Searchers identified the body by an unopened letter to his wife found in a breast pocket of his distinctive tweed jacket. An autopsy is planned to determine the cause of death."

ME, YELLING AT TV: "I'd say the cause of death was pretty clearly trying to climb Everest in a tweed jacket!"

Anyway, met Eva our lawyer at city hall and then Erika the interpreter. (A certified interpreter is required at such signings, lest unsuspecting Americans sign documents agreeing to tuck-point city hall. Working with Erika has been a highlight of our experience. We'd adopt her too, except she's like 30.)

First stop was the office of a county official, a 50-ish woman with hair dyed Morticia-black and shaped like a football helmet. She seems to admire what we have done and pulled several strings to get me out of here a little early.

Then it was off to the guy who types birth certificates (one finger at a time, on a manual typewriter) for a living. When I grow up I want this job. When we got to the door, we saw office hours for Friday were listed as "ninc" which is "none." Eva, a dynamo of a woman, 40-ish with short hair and large glasses, sighed and pounded on the metal door. No answer. Again, **BOOM BOOM BOOM.**

Nothing. So she tries the door. It opens and she gestures us to follow. (I wait a fraction of a second for a shotgun blast.) Hearing none, I step forward to see Eva talking to the clerk, gesturing wildly. He clearly does not want to do anything today.

After 10 minutes of jabbering she convinces him somehow (I do not want to know how) and I am gestured to take a seat, asked for my passport and he begins to type with two fingers. About 45 minutes and 3,000 Forints ($13) later I have Cary's Hungarian birth certificate listing Kim and I as his parents.

After a quick lunch, I headed to the fruit stand to clean them out of bananas and other fruit (the stand-owner sees me coming and bows) and then rushed to the orphanage for the farewell party. The caregivers there had dressed all of the kids in special clothes, including a newborn that had arrived there two hours before to take Cary's place. (It's so sad to see that as fast as the kids get out of that place another one arrives to fill the spot.)

Yoshi also was there, just sitting in his bed, looking sad. Kati had told him I was leaving with Cary today and he was taking it very hard. (I had asked several times about his status; turns out he was an "economic orphan" in that his parents or parent still wanted him but could not afford to raise him.)

Parents of "economic orphans" get to visit Thursday mornings and Sunday afternoons in the lobby of the orphanage. Visitation day is a gut-wrenching thing to see; I tried to avoid it every opportunity. It mainly consists of parents older than their years huddled in the corners of the room trying to stay connected with their kids in 15-minute blocks of time. It's truly horrible.

I was really loaded down with fruit and other stuff and it was a good feeling to see the faces of the kids when they saw the loot. (If you want to impress a little kid, show up with 200 Milky Way bars, 4,000 butter cookies, 150 bananas and 100 "Balaton" candy bars.)

Yoshi finally got off his bed and joined in. Cary was resplendent in some overalls and a baseball jacket we had brought from the States. The kids gathered around for a pudding cake that Kati had made, which was wolfed down. Cary's friend, little Eva, Yoshi and an absolutely stunning little girl whose name I cannot spell, then got the balloons out and whacked them around a bit.

I gave out some gifts and photos to the caregivers and to the staff, who seemed genuinely surprised. I can't stress how hard a job this is, 15 hours a day, 27 days a month, $125 a month in pay. This is with eight kids per room, including two or three infants. (At night they have cut back to one caregiver per 30 kids.)

Another orphanage farewell scene

More last-minute papers were signed, documents exchanged and then it was time to go. I thought I survived it but then someone got the brilliant idea that "everyone" should see us out to the door. I thought they meant the door of the room; they meant the front gate of the orphanage. I picked up Cary and walked slowly down the hall with him, again rubbing his head in the plants on the wall while singing "Baby Bumblebee." Then it hit me I did exactly the same thing, with the same song, with Kristian, the day we left with the four. I looked into Cary's face and Kristian smiled back and I just lost it. Our friend Edit helped me make it out of the place and I finally gave Cary back to Kati, who murmured softly to him in Hungarian down the rest of the long, long hall.

I fled into the foyer, then saw the empty incubator right inside the front door and I honestly barely made it to the car. Then Yoshi came up and hugged my leg as I unloaded stuff into the car. I gave him a toy I had been saving for him and a big bag of cookies. I dropped to my knees and felt each of his fingers on my back during a terribly long, painful hug. I told him to be a good boy and that I was proud of him and he was hustled back. Edit pried Cary out of Kati's hands and I gave each staffer a hug and two kisses. Then a hug and kiss to the other six kids, three of whom were wailing.

Cary's first meal of freedom

I headed to the refuge of the car and got it started, while Edit and Cary clambered into the back seat. With a wave and lots of "szias" I moved slowly down the dirt road. I could not go too fast because I didn't want to raise a cloud of dust, but I wanted — needed — to get out of there like Mario Andretti. I *willed myself not to look in the rearview mirror because I knew it would be one of those images seared into my soul. But like passing a car wreck on the interstate, I glanced anyway and saw the weeping teachers and children all waving, standing in the middle of the dusty road.*

It's a good thing my small hotel was right there, so I peeled in there and Edit occupied Cary in the lobby while I lost my mind in the room for a bit.

As hard as it was, I really value my time in the orphanage. It is where the children came from and an important part of their background. We can answer nearly any question my kids could come up with about their early childhood. And I know we are doing a good thing by taking children out of there. But boy is it hard.

The three of us ate dinner in a Hungarian inn that Edit found and Cary loved the violin player that kept coming to the table. (I was prepared to tip him heavily to stay away.)

After we got home from the inn, I put Cary to bet in the chilly hotel room. I finally got him to sleep after about 15 minutes of fussing. It's hard to believe as I am writing this my snoring son is spending his first night outside of an institution.

I wish I knew what he was thinking.

CHAPTER 27: Cary's new life starts

From: Jamesderk@aol.com
Date: 16 May 1999 19:14:53 -0400 (EDT)
To:Dad (wderk@aol.com)
Subject: New life

Cary woke up about 6 a.m., yawned and grinned at me. As I picked him up and cuddled with him, I whispered, "today is the first day of the rest of your life." (Considering he is 18 months old and doesn't speak English, no way he will recognize it as a cereal jingle.)

Today was my first full day as Mister Mom with Cary and we did famously. Last night was a bit scary; Cary has had respiratory problems all week and once I got him to sleep here at the hotel he was happily snoring for a while. But later I heard this rhythm where he would rasp five breaths, then stop breathing completely for about 10 seconds, then wake up gasping. It was classic sleep apnea and it scared the heck out of me. I woke him up enough to get a suppository of this Hungarian croup medicine in him. His breathing did improve somewhat, but I was awake most of the night just listening to him breathe.

After playing for a few hours, we padded down to breakfast in the inn. Cary ate gobs of Hungarian bread slathered with jam, which I think was a first for him.

We then went outside for a walk, mostly to get him used to the stroller, which I will need in various airports. He's hated riding in it before, but this time I sat him in it and, before he could react, filled his lap with Pukis, these corn curl things with the taste and consistency of packing popcorn.

By the time he realized he was in the stroller (a block from the hotel), he seemed to be able to tolerate it. So we wandered around the neighborhood, the same one Kim and I walked endlessly with the four kids, watching houses under construction.

There can't be any kind of building codes here; the level of construction is hilarious. One house I saw consists of straw bales wrapped together with stucco slathered over it. (I think the "Three Little Pigs" must not have been translated into Hungarian.)

Anyway, we walked around the rear of the orphanage property but I didn't have the stomach to come within sight of it again. We must have made about 15 laps of the neighborhood. After that we parked ourselves at a bus stop and watched big buses come and go.

Nearly everyone uses public transportation here, so there were dozens and dozens of buses and all categories of people to watch. (For some reason most women under 30 here have dyed their hair a sort of burgundy so I got a kick out of that.) We petted a stray dog or two and headed back to the room to get ready for lunch.

I had no idea what to order him in the small dining room but the waiter took one look at us when we sat down and brought me three Cokes and some ham and three bowls of something for Cary. Whatever it was, he liked it and I appreciated the help from the waiter.

Then it was nap time. I strapped him in his szack (on loan from the orphanage because it is so cold in the hotel) and he just sighed and laid down. It was unreal

I turned on the TV and just caught a report of the BBC's wine critic, one Jancis Robinson, describe a particular wine as "reeking of cat's pee on a gooseberry bush."

(I do so love a good turn of phrase.)

He slept almost three hours showing me he was not getting enough sleep under the orphanage's rigid system. (Plus, once one kid was up in the room in the morning, they all were awakened by the resulting chaos).

At 3:30 he yawned and sat up. We did the diaper gig again (Pampers are so much easier than the cloth ones in the orphanage) and headed back out in the stroller. Heading nowhere in particular, we happened to run into a massive street fair. The whole fair was a bunch of vendor tents and people were clambering for access to the stuff.

I am not claustrophobic but I needed to get out of the mob, so we parked ourselves in front of some street musicians on a makeshift stage. Cary clapped along to the beat and when they finished, I walked over to tip one of the olive-skinned men and said, "He loves Gypsy music." The man smiled and said, "I do too, but we are from Peru!"

I walked another block and detoured behind the stalls to get away from the crowd when I was approached by an attractive, too-made-up young woman. Talking rapidly to me in Hungarian, she then tried to take my arm. Two thoughts rushed my mind at this point: 1) this is a lady of the evening and 2) I am pushing a baby in a stroller. The second thought sort of erased thought No. 1, but I faced a dilemma. I had literally no idea what she was asking me.

My response options were "Nem Kerem," sort of a polite but illiterate "No thank you." Great answer for No. 1, but then I figured what if she's asking me directions to the bathroom? I settled on "Et Nem Magyar" a rudimentary "I am not Hungarian." She responded with a large smile and a "yo" (OK) and a gesture to follow her. I opted to wave and make a left turn back to the throng.

One block later, another young woman tapped me on the shoulder and said, "You're American, right?" Here we go again, I am thinking. This teen ends up being a missionary from California, part of a group traveling from orphanage to orphanage across Eastern Europe. (I am continually busted as American because of my Nike shoes and my baseball cap. One Hungarian woman earlier had asked me "why do you always wear a little boy's hat?")

I shared with the teen my Cliff's Notes version of our adoption story and filled her in on some of our experiences. I have a lot of respect for young people who give up their summers to make a difference in the world instead of hanging out at the mall. She said they had not been to the Debrecen orphanage yet but the others across Hungary were considered excellent in comparison to most of the rest of Europe. I was happy to share what I knew and it was nice to know the orphanage system here was pretty well maintained.

It was time to flee; so, Cary and I strolled back to the hotel and headed to the dining room for dinner. This time the waiter (the same one...apparently their shifts run around the clock) brought us rolled turkey, tomatoes so red you could see the sun in every one, and various mixed veggies.

Cary ate a lot and we had the whole place to ourselves. (He and I usually ate supper at the American dinner time and most Europeans don't even sit down for dinner until 9 p.m. or later.)

Then it was bath time, the first outside of the orphanage. Cary cried a little because of the size of the tub but we made it a quickie and he was fine.

We played for a few more minutes and then it was time for bed -- more amazingly I strapped him into his szack and laid him down. He started sucking his thumb and that was it. Not a peep.

Daddy be thankful.

I got to call home to America to Brandon to see how he was doing with his newly diagnosed Chickenpox and shared a too-brief time with him. Also talked to Kim and the other kids; they all seem so far away.

I miss everyone.

Tomorrow I pack and leave for the hotel in Budapest, so we can at least be closer to the papers that will let us get out of here. Our business in Debrecen is done.

I can't wait to show Cary the world.

CHAPTER 28: Budapest or bust

Once again with the help of Edit, I headed to Budapest with a new Hungarian child. This whole adventure could not have been accomplished without her. Not only did she bridge the language barrier, but her knowledge of the kids and the country made her invaluable to me.

In Budapest, I got a small room (maybe 10 x 10) on the rooftop of a small hotel on a side street. The room had a very large, uncovered skylight window, so the next morning started at 5:40 A.M. when my little guy figured it was bright enough in our rooftop room that it must be time to get up.

He woke me up and probably everyone in the hotel, as the walls were made of Kleenex and spit. It was just as well; at 6 A.M., the city's garbage men decided to empty a trash bin full of bricks down on the street -- you have not heard a sound as loud as a thousand bricks hitting an empty metal garbage truck at six in the morning.

I tried amusing Cary to stall until breakfast time, but in our little room there was not much to do. So at 7 we headed to the hotel restaurant and played a new game called "throw everything on the floor."

(Actually, he played the game, I got the parting gifts.)

Luckily we were the only ones actually eating at that hour, so we didn't ruin mealtime for anyone else.

Edit and her sister then came over, and we went for a "walk," which in Hungary means a brisk three miles or so. These people walk everywhere.

Budapest is really an amazing city; if not for the grime and the graffiti, it would truly live up to its name "The Paris of the East."

People who live in Budapest must take all of the history for granted. It's not at all amusing to them that a Pizza Hut is ensconced in a building constructed in 1711. Buildings here that are used for ordinary things would be surrounded by velvet ropes and armed guards in the United States.

After a quick pizza, we rushed back to the hotel to meet Eva, our lawyer, who handed over Cary's passport and a bunch of other documents, right on time. (However the Hungarian legal system works, Eva can play it like a fiddle.)

Armed with my new documents I ran over to the American Embassy with one cranky, napless child and found an absolute throng waiting outside. Most of them were Yugoslavians waiting for tomorrow's opening of the embassy for visa applications. They will wait all night in line.

Showing my American passport got us to the front of the line, which was manned by grim U.S. Marines with assault weapons. Once inside I met our contact behind the bulletproof window, and we passed documents back and forth for about a half hour. I was, of course, two documents short, but whatever they were, she let me fill them out on the spot. One required Kim's signature, a pretty good trick considering she was in Indiana at the time. I "forgot" to mention it and the clerk never noticed when I passed it back.

About two hours later, an inch-thick, sealed packet slid out the window, and Cary was granted permanent resident alien status in the good old U.S. of A. (When you get a visa you don't actually get to see much of it. The materials are securely sealed in an envelope that must be presented still sealed to the INS folks upon arrival in the United States. You only see the cover page with the immigrant's photo on it.) If you open it, you go to jail. Really, it says that right on the front.

Welcome to America. Tear this envelope and you're under arrest.

On the way out, an old couple who had been conversing in a corner of the room emerged; he was beaming, and she was weeping. Both were clutching American visas. He saw one in my hand and gestured to his. His wife grabbed my arm and showed me hers. Both of them were from Yugoslavia and both had been granted permission to travel to America. They jabbered some stuff that I couldn't understand, waved, and tottered off.

I felt both elation and a terrible smugness that I take being an American too much for granted. The line outside had grown two-fold while we were in there.

To celebrate Cary's visa we picked up Edit, jumped in the car and headed to Gellért Hill above Budapest where Hungary has what it calls its Statue of Liberty, a monument that soars on Angel's wings and honors Hungary's liberation from the Germans after World War II. The hill is named after Bishop Gerald Gellért, the country's first Christian martyr who was rolled down the hill in a barrel of spikes in 1046. (I am digressing here but have we as a society killed people in some pretty odd ways??)

Surrounding the statue is an ancient fort that is pockmarked with thousands of bullets and shells. The Germans used it for a strategic post during World War II, and the Russians spent months trying to capture it, sustaining huge losses. Russia finally got the fort, and the country, but never quite got around to leaving for 45 years.

The Russian occupation was brought home to me when I stopped at the souvenir stand and tried on a surplus Russian army hat. For five bucks I thought it would be pretty darn funny to wear home on the plane.

I got a frosty look from Edit and she said, "Jim, you American. Russia big funny. Russia not funny when Russia in your country 40 years and no go home."

Point taken. I put the hat back.

It had been a good trip in that regard. I will never again moan when I have to manually start my lawn mower after watching a guy mow acres of grass with a sickle.

CHAPTER 29: Cary's Medical Misadventures

Budapest is lovely, but it's tough to get around. My hotel was in Buda and the doctor Cary had to see was in Pest, across the Danube River. (Budapest actually is made up of three separate cities: Buda, Óbuda and Pest).

The trouble with getting around is, when Buda and Pest were built in the 12th century, the planners amazingly did not plan for cars and trucks. The streets in the Downtown area are all one-way and all Pinewood Derby narrow.

Thanks to help from Edit I actually found the hospital and a place to park, which was a stunning achievement in navigation. (When I turned off the car, I turned to Edit and said, "Tranquility Base here, the Eagle has landed" to which Edit replied, "Eagle? What is eagle?")

I then found the correct room number in the hospital's office wing (mental note: NEVER GET SICK IN HUNGARY) where the doctor told me to meet him. Like normal in the U.S., I opened the door and expected to find a receptionist and a waiting room. Instead I found a partly naked woman undergoing an exam. Ooops.

Lesson 1: In Hungary, a doctor's office is one room. When a doctor tells you to meet him in Room 201, you don't actually go in. You wait in the hallway until the doctor finds you. A few minutes later, the doctor comes out and it turns out to be the same guy who examined our other four kids in Budapest in 1997. It was nice to see him again.

He gave Cary a cursory exam, then asked for the medical form we got from the American Embassy. I checked my folder with 1,000 forms in it (I never left the house without a satchel full of documents) but could not find the one he needed. Without it, he said, he could not approve Cary's admission to the United States. It was far too late in the day to get back to the Embassy to get another one.

I visibly sagged, but he told me to wait, disappeared for a couple minutes and came back with the magic blank form. "I always keep a spare," he said.

Then he asked when Cary had his Hepatitis B shots in the orphanage. I said I asked to have him vaccinated for that, but the Hungarian doctor refused to give the shots because she thought Cary was too young. Turns out, of course, the Hungarian doctor was wrong, and Cary can't enter the United States until he has three shots, 24 hours apart. That would put me another week in Hungary.

I looked like my puppy was drowned at that point. The doctor again took pity on me. He asked, "Do you promise to have this done when you get home?" I nearly hugged the guy.

He scribbled something in Hungarian on some form, slapped a bunch of seals on it, and we were on our way back to the hotel and our rooftop room. I peered out the window at the city below and thought about going home soon. (Out our window I could see a church built in the 13th century complete with 200 pigeons pooping on it.)

On this trip I also saw Hungarian storks that make nests the size of Volkswagens on top of the power poles. They just look stupid, like Big Bird sitting on a fake nest. The whole thing is so out of proportion, just so "wrong" that I laughed every time I saw one. The whole mess is precariously balanced on the top of a pole, so if the bird leans wrong, the whole thing must go over the side.

On our last visit here, Kim and I had to rush through Budapest. I doubt we spent more than 36 hours here. This time we had lots of time, just Cary and me, so we spent many days just wandering around the city. (Being a Chicago native, city life is in my genes.)

The whole city is gorgeous in a museum sort of way. Everything above the first floor of every building is gorgeous. However, the first floor of nearly every building is covered in graffiti. I saw the city workers trying to remove it but it's a shame people have no respect for beauty.

One night after a quick dinner, I put Cary in the stroller and we walked about three miles downtown, looking at buildings and the people. It is so apparent that I am American that during our stroll, two "Rendorsheg" (police) officers in paramilitary gear walked over to me. I am thinking, "Papers!" again, but instead one of the officers says, "Welcome to Budapest" in perfect English and hands Cary a candy bar.

Never again will I get to spend so much time alone with one of my children so that was a big plus.

It had been a great time with all of the sightseeing and all, but the time had come. The next day we were going to try to get out of there.

CHAPTER 31: Heading home, again

Making any kind of transcontinental airplane flight these days is no fun; making one with a baby is extremely unpleasant. However, you're talking a whole 'nother world when you take a long trip with a child where every single thing he sees is new to him.

They become victims of what Kim and I dubbed "sensory overload." I thought the flight with the first four was intense but at least I had Kim with me. This time I had to do it by myself.

When we arrived at the Budapest airport, I had most everything under control. I returned the rental car without a hitch, conned Cary into using the stroller and, with Edit's help, got our four bags to the terminal with an hour to spare.

Twice Hungarian military or customs officials, who no doubt have never seen an adoptive father traveling alone, politely interrogated me. Each time I presented Cary's inch-thick, sealed immigration folder. It was carefully examined, and we were allowed to pass. Considering there are only a handful of adoptions there every year it must have been pretty unusual.

By this time, Cary and I were pretty fast friends, which helped. I can't imagine having to drag some unwilling toddler through an airport. Instead he was rather openly affectionate. That is, until we cleared security and headed to the hold room, where Cary threw one incredible temper tantrum when I rather politely suggested he shouldn't break everything in the airport gift shop.

Luckily, the flight attendants took pity on me as I boarded the Malev Airlines jet with my still whining child and my one ticket in coach. (Despite our unpleasant experiences last time with a "lap baby" we had done it again. We simply could not afford the $1,000 for a seat for Cary.)

A flight attendant met me half-way down the jet-bridge, and I suddenly found my seat moved to the bulkhead (more legroom). When I sat down I found that the plane's only vacant seat had been moved next to me. (At that moment I vowed to marry a flight attendant in my next life...they have been the absolutely nicest people on our whole adventure.)

Of course, Cary never actually *sat* in the seat for the entire 12-hour first leg, but it was nice that someone would not have to sit directly next to my soon-to-be screaming child.

Once we pushed back from the gate, Cary amazingly fell dead asleep on my lap. This, by the way, had never happened before. I felt like I had won the lottery. As I was cheering internally for having at least two hours of the trip smooth as gravy, the pilot came on the intercom and announced loudly in three languages (*shhhh, can't you see the baby is sleeping!!!*) that all air traffic was being held so a group of American warplanes could use the runways.

So, we sat on the taxiway for about 90 minutes watching the roaring American jets shoot off the runways before we were finally allowed to leave. As our wheels left the runway and went **THUNK** into their slots in the fuselage, my son awoke with a start.

The flight from Budapest to New York was a blur of thrown food, screaming and tears. (And that was just *me!*) Cary simply was a blur of activity and none too keen about staying in our little bulkhead area. I'd put my legs up to block him from walking out into the aisle, he'd crawl under. I'd put them down, he'd crawl over. I'd block both, he'd cry. I'd try games, puzzles, stuffed animals, books, music, blocks, snacks, water, juice....

I am not sure I was even present for some of it. I know the bulk of the trip was spent with me walking laps; down the aisle, through the back galley, up the other aisle and through that galley, then back down again.

Upon landing in New York, we had about two hours to make our flight to Cincinnati. About an hour of that was spent clearing Immigration. I'll never forget the look of the officer when he scanned my passport into the computer and my profile popped on the screen; he did a double take, looked at me and asked how the first four kids were coming along. He passed me back my passport, grinning, and said, "You people are nuts."

About an hour later Cary was declared a "Permanent Resident Alien," and we were on our way to Cincinnati. On that two-hour flight, thankfully, I sat next to two moms traveling without their kids. They both fought over holding Cary, which was a nice respite for me.

In Cincinnati, we had to take an airport tram and a bus before finally boarding the final flight to Evansville. Cary seemingly shared my affection for the rubber band-powered commuter plane and tossed another fit, which lasted until the stale pretzels arrived.

I confess, I'd never been quite so happy to fly over Evansville as I was that night. Once the propellers stopped, I bounded out of the plane and hauled the now-drowsy Cary up the steps into the terminal. We were immediately tackled by the other kids and my wife, who scooped up our new son.

"I got him home, you raise him," I quipped, handing him over.

Our daughter, Ava, kept pointing to Cary and calling him "Addie," her pet name for Adam, her twin brother. She spent the first few minutes as we rolled around on the airport carpet just totally confused as to why there now were two Adams in her life. She was right; the resemblance was pretty scary once they were side by side. Because Cary is big for his age and Adam small, they do look like twins.

Finally, it seemed, we were all together and we could start putting our lives back together on the same continent.

CHAPTER 32: We are family

Our lives clearly changed with the arrival of yet another toddler. We sold our "small" seven-passenger van and bought a used 15-passenger church bus so our whole family could go someplace at the same time. With five kids in car seats and the accompanying baby paraphernalia, sometimes even the bus wasn't big enough.

Cary became immersed in the family nearly immediately. Ava just assumed he was her baby, so we sort of had to explain that one away over time. He arrived with some orphanage behaviors, including biting, that created havoc in our family (not to mention increased our expenditures in bandages and salve). Both Adam and Ava took that as one behavior to emulate, making some days at our home appear to be a bad Dracula movie.

Cary arrived with the same medical problems as the others; he was diagnosed immediately with two raging ear infections and huge tonsils. Dr. Logan took care of Cary within the first week, and his scary apnea was gone, too.

Believe it or not, Kim and I were still hanging in there despite some pretty long days (and nights). By then the only real casualty was sleep -- we were not getting very much of it. That, and we didn't have very much "grown-up time" to be a couple. We didn't have much money for sitters, we had no local extended family and we were not spending much time alone.

But we were enjoying the time we had as a family. We had some pretty odd experiences along the way.

On Aug. 1, we decided to hold a "mass Baptism" for our new five at Bethlehem United Church of Christ. I joked during the ceremony that the

Rev. Scott Keehn could use a super soaker and get the whole group at once. He suggested he felt like Sun Myung Moon doing a mass wedding. Having all of our children join the world of God together with our families and their sponsors was not a moment we will ever forget.

And we took everyone to Disney World (in a 30-foot RV no less) a move that boldly supported our friends' contention we were potentially insane. Motoring down the interstate it was easy to look in the mirror and feel more than a little overwhelmed with it all. What was a guy like me doing with all of this responsibility? But it would only take a hug from Ava or a drawing from Willie and everything would be okay again.

And we did feel blessed. Despite what everyone kept telling us, we knew we were not doing something special for these kids; they were doing something special for us.

Adam, Cary, Willie. Dad, Brandon, Kim, Ava, Coleen and Kristian, in 2000

CHAPTER 33: You have *got* to be kidding

One of the best things to come out our adventure was that our story (as printed in a series of stories in *The Evansville Courier & Press*) inspired others to adopt children. We heard from dozens of couples that the stories actually encouraged them to take the plunge themselves. That was incredibly heartwarming. One couple, Harold & Darla Grossman, actually traveled back to Hungary to adopt a little girl from the same city.

During their adoption trip to Hungary in 2000, Harold Grossman was on a bus in Debrecen one day, and overheard some women talking in Hungarian. He was surprised to hear our last name in the conversation. When he asked his interpreter what the people were talking about, the interpreter reported that they were discussing how sad it was that there was yet another baby in the orphanage with the same parents as the Derk children

Harold sent me an e-mail reporting what he'd heard and almost simultaneously we received a call from János with the news we'd been expecting: a baby girl was waiting in Debrecen. Did we want her, too?

Baby would make eight… almost a baseball team.

This was another huge decision for Kim and I to make and raised the same questions we'd had with Cary. Was bringing home yet another child fair to the kids we already had? Was there enough parenting left in our bones for eight? Are we just moving the orphanage here?

We talked about it alone for a few hours, but what is there really to say? There's no way we could afford it (we'd only paid off the loans for one of the original five kids by this point), the house wasn't big enough, we were already stressed beyond belief, *yadda, yadda.*

But of course, the decision wasn't really a decision. We knew we could not leave a sibling of our children in an orphanage in Eastern Europe. We held a family meeting and talked to the kids about it. They couldn't believe it, of course, and voted unanimously for us to bring her home. Ava was the most excited of all, to have a baby sister.

We called János back and told him to start the coaster down the huge track again.

We called the social worker to update our home study again to strains of *"you have to be kidding."* The social worker visited the house, found we were still doing okay and updated our home study in about a week. We took a long breath and faxed the revision to Hungary.

Despite this being a sibling to our children, there was no guarantee the petition for adoption would be granted. Though Hungarian law made it a requirement to notify us of the birth (with the goal of family unification) this was not a slam-dunk. If anything we were going to have to work harder to convince the Hungarians that two middle-aged people can raise eight children.

Again we pleaded with the U.S. Immigration & Naturalization Service to speed up the processing of our paperwork…surely as *five-time* international adoption veterans they would work with us and help us get this little girl home in a timely manner. Surely, we thought, they would pull out all of the stops and help a little girl be reunited with her brothers and sisters.

Well, no. This time the INS was even *less* helpful than before. They even decided our fingerprints, taken three or four times before and still on file in three separate INS offices, somehow must have changed and we needed new ones. (This is a huge deal because the INS does not accept fingerprints taken from any other agency, including local police or the FBI. They require the prints to be taken in an INS office. That's lovely, but there isn't one in my city and that meant a seven-hour round-trip drive to the office in Indianapolis just to have this done.)

On the Hungarian side, we asked the caseworkers there to visit the girl's birth parents and see if they would be willing to sign away their parental rights before the 12-month waiting period. That would allow her to leave the country as soon as the INS approved us and maybe get her out of the orphanage a few months sooner.

However, the biological father got violent with the caseworkers and refused to help. That meant we had to wait until she was at least one year old to file our official petition. Then, and only then, would the INS start its side of the paperwork.

Edit holding Kristiana, one of the first photos we received

So it was another six months before we could get clearance to come take our daughter, named Krisztiana, out of the orphanage. Yes, this time it took the INS a half-year to report (surprise!) that we were **STILL** not felons. Another inch of paperwork later we applied to Hungary for a final hearing.

We nearly lost the baby girl in the long INS process: another couple had inquired about her and we were still waiting on American approval. The Hungarian government thought we had to be stalling... surely it would not take this long for the INS to approve. János managed to convince them that the delay was not on our end.

But after a ton of money and frayed nerves we found ourselves on a plane – again – heading to Budapest. The Hungarians had not agreed to waive the residency requirement (again) so Kim and I decided to "tag-team" the month, both spending some time in country and then taking turns staying in Hungary. It wasn't ideal but it was the only way we could work it out. Kim's parents again agreed to cover us back home, which was a life-saver.

My diary at the time had the following entry:

The trip went like clockwork. Every plane was on time. The Amsterdam airport is amazing...the cleanest public place I have ever seen. Our takeoff from Amsterdam to Budapest aboard a 737 with about 12 people on it was hilarious and terrifying. In dense fog that would have grounded every plane in the USA, the pilot floored the throttles and took off at about an 80-degree angle. My cheeks were pulled back into my face like that guy in LIFE magazine.

We landed in Budapest, rented our car and drove three hours to Debrecen and checked into the Derk suite at the Park Hotel. In a stunning development, we sat down for lunch and the waiter brought us six Cokes. It's nice to be remembered. The staff is totally floored that we are back, again, for another child.

Frankly, so are we.

The next morning we met with the orphanage leaders (again) and had a tearful reunion with members of the staff. We showed all kinds of photographs of the other kids and they marveled at how big they have grown.

We are using Erika for our interpreter this time...the more-expensive firepower of János isn't needed in person. (If this keeps up we won't need an interpreter at all by kid # 16.)

After a short discussion with the orphanage staff it was time for another long, heart-rending walk down the same hallways. Turns out she also was being raised in the same room as Willie and the twins. When we opened the door we finally got to meet Krisztiana; she was an absolute doll. Blonde, very curly hair, never been cut, big blue eyes. She looked at us for a second then walked right into my arms and held tight. (Call it the "anti-Cary reaction")

She is an exact match for the other kids…a mixture of Adam with a little Willie and Kris tossed in. She showed no resistance in bonding with us…at one point she just sat in my lap and grabbed my index fingers with a death grip and just sagged into my arms. She's very cuddly and loving. She loves her bath and kicking her feet.

She's still a bit unsteady walking, but appears to spend a lot of time being cuddled by the caregivers. (Because there is no "sz" letter in English, we changed her name to Kristiana, with a middle name of Julia in honor of my fraternal grandmother.)

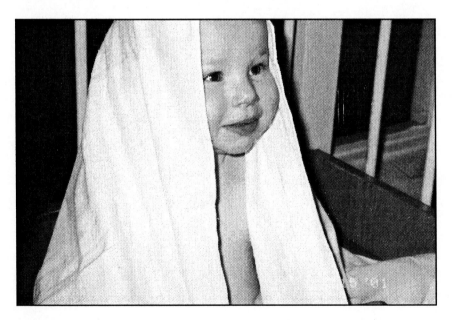

Kristiana at bath time

After wolfing down her lunch of steamed cabbage (!), applesauce and juice, she was packed into a "szack" and hat and placed outside to sleep, despite a head cold and 42-degree weather outside. Needless to say, we're looking forward to getting her out of there as soon as possible even if we can't get her out of the country quite yet. It appears we will get custody on Monday and then we will head to a hotel in Budapest until the American Embassy says we can go home.

Our visit to the Embassy the next day went well but we could not help but notice the change in security; the whole Embassy is now ringed with metal fencing and blast doors. Grim-faced Marines (are there other kinds?) check under each car with a mirror before letting any pass anywhere near. It appears our papers are in order and now we wait for someone to sign them.

That could be in 24 minutes or 24 days, you never know with the American government.

We're doing our best to keep our heads.

CHAPTER 34: Making tracks

The official court hearings in Debrecen went very well, primarily because so many of the officials remembered us from the previous visits. We thought they would give us trouble about adopting our 8th child, but János had done a great job greasing the skids and it was a brief hearing with Erika doing all of the talking for us. (I imagine by this time they had run out of questions about our mental capacity.)

Our hinge in getting out of there in a timely manner was whether the birth certificate office would issue three, hand-typed certificates on the same day. Turns out a grumpy woman was the only one working there, and she wasn't inclined to turn around the needed documents quickly. I grabbed Kristiana from Kim's arms in the hallway and carried her in, looking all blonde and curly. That worked like a charm. The lady took pity on us and, amazingly, made all the certificates while we waited, just like last time, *tap, tap, tap on* a manual typewriter. I did see some computers in the office this time, which should be a big step forward if they ever use them.

We woke up early the next day to head to the Hungarian passport office, where a kind woman extracted a small fee and our signatures and said Kristie's passport would ready in a week.

Our only missing piece was the person at the American Embassy who handles adoptions. She has been on vacation and has no idea we are here, despite our leaving numerous messages. We walked over to the Embassy today after they refused to answer the phone and left her a note asking for an appointment for 1:30 P.M. Monday.

The Embassy was again crowded with Yugoslavians seeking asylum in the USA but we got in and out okay.

The next day the real chaos started. János called from Hawaii to say the American Embassy called him and wanted additional documents from us. In one case, they had the Hungarian translation of a document that we'd faxed while we were still in the States. Turns out we needed TWO copies of the original English versions, but no one told us. That could be cleared up -- János was going to FedEx them the originals.

The second issue turned out to be huge... the Hungarian government now decided they wanted us to have medical clearance – something that we hadn't been told about. Basically the Hungarians wanted our doctors at home to certify that we were physically fit to be parents and we would not drop dead a week after getting Kristie home.

We thought we'd call our American doctors back home and have them certify we were physically fit. After all, Kim and I have routine annual physicals and all of our records could be faxed over in a jiffy. No good, said the Hungarians. They wanted a fresh examination.

Our only answer -- go to a Hungarian doctor. The next day we found find ourselves at this tiny clinic somewhere outside Debrecen. (Edit helped us find it.) We stepped through the office door and back at least five decades, if not more. It looked just like a movie set, complete with cloth screens splattered with something that we dared not ask about and a huge Russian radio made during the Truman administration.

The room was no bigger than an average American living room and was packed with the examining area, the doctor's files and two dour-looking women behind big steel institutional desks. We were, however, greeted by the most sweet-faced doctor we'd ever met. He looked like he came straight of Central Casting. He ushered us over to his examination area, took a look at the medical documents we'd brought, asked a couple of health questions and said he was done.

We had been warned that we'd have to pay cash for his services because we obviously weren't covered under Hungary's national health program. But he'd have none of it. He dictated the precious authorization to his clerk, who typed it up on the spot. After arguing with him to take a small fee, we finally agreed that we'd make a donation to the orphanage in his name to cover his time.

(It's moments like this that remind us that no matter where we live on Earth, most people are really trying to do the right thing. He had a real opportunity to "take the Americans" but he chose to just help instead.)

We finally got back to Kristiana in time for her evening bath, and she seemed glad to see us. She waddled over to me and plopped down on my lap, then relaxed against me with a big sigh. She was perfectly content to sit like this for hours. She seemed much different than the other children in that she's amazingly relaxed; not a tense muscle in her body. It's like having a little doll on your lap.

Kristie and her rosy cheeks

Kim was able to feed her lunch and give her a bath in the short time we were there today. In fact, Kristie was quite active despite she's not feeling well at all. Her doctor gave her some heavy-duty antibiotics and some cold medicine, in hopes of getting her cleared up before we can take her out of the orphanage for good.

One last major hurdle to get through: János must deliver on a promise to get the original documents to the orphanage director via FedEx.

If they didn't show up, then we were toast for another week.

CHAPTER 35: Home stretch

One morning after waking up at the Hotel Park, we scooted over to the orphanage and found Kristiana dressed like the cover of a Hungarian folklore calendar, with amazingly bright red cheeks. While she looked adorable, it turned out that the cheeks were the visual clue that her cold wasn't getting any better. She again wasn't interested in playing, preferring instead to sit as long as possible on our laps.

Within a half an hour or so, she proved that while she may look just like several of her brothers, she was going to be quite different in other respects. With little fuss, she settled into my arms and went to sleep. This is the first one of the children that has been able to fall asleep in our arms. While I was sure it had something to do with her not feeling well, it still was a huge surprise. We were not counting on it sticking around forever, but it had been really nice as we were trying to bond with her as quickly as possible.

After her nap, I got a chance to feed her something that looked absolutely disgusting, but she gobbled up. Then I bundled her into her little sleep sack and bonnet and put her into her crib outside.

When we returned after the nap we were rewarded by Kristiana taking off across the room toward us with a huge smile on her face. She stopped for a hug from Kim, then pushed past to get one from me.

We played for the afternoon, just hanging around. She ate something for dinner that I think was beetroot sauce mixed with sour cream. (*Where do they get this stuff?*) We spent the next several hours falling more deeply in love with our newest daughter, who had been given some medicine that took the red out of cheeks and helped her breathe easier. It was a fun day, with all of us discovering what games made her smile and which ones made her turn up her nose. She also has a facial expression that is unique to her; when she's contemplating something very seriously, she lifts her right eyebrow. Such a grown-up expression on such a little face.

Finally she snuggled up onto Kim's shoulder and went to sleep again before bath time and snack. She apparently thought the goal of bath time is to get as much water outside of the bathtub as quickly as possible, and she was very good at it. Within moments, Kim was drenched and Kristie was laughing a high-pitched giggle.

Her caregiver, a different woman named Kati (pronounced COT-tee), said via sign language that bath is her favorite activity of the day; we definitely believed it. She stayed in a good mood for the rest of the evening.

It was still very hard on Kim and I to be in the orphanage. As has happened every time we'd come here, we couldn't remain detached from the other children.

While Kim was giving Kristiana a bath, I responded to some cries coming from the other room. Soon I was sitting on the old rug with children on each knee and a couple more trying to get close. In front of me rolled a tiny little boy who is at least three years old, but mentally disabled. (During our very first visit here, he was the little baby that they were debating if he was "worth" heart surgery). He was still there.

Two of the children are sisters who were so malnourished and in such poor health, that it's impossible to believe they are 2 and 3 years old.

There's another little Gypsy boy who has quietly captured my heart again. He's about Kristiana's age, and the first day he saw me, he toddled over and smiled this huge smile. He is one of seven children brought to live in the orphanage while his mother is in jail. There were three infants in this room too – two who are five months old and one who is just three months. They're tiny, adorable and rarely held, primarily because the older children demand the attention. All three have lost their hair in the back from laying their backs for so long and rocking their heads to get to sleep. They respond to the slightest touch by wiggling as close as they can.

I kept thinking that this trip should be the easiest, but for us it was by far the hardest. While Hungarian "life" in general appears to be improving for many people (we're amazed at the "trappings" that have sprung up in the last three years – the stores, pubs, etc.) life doesn't appear to be getting any better for Hungary's children. The orphanage remained full and, while there were toys and things around, people were telling us that fewer prospective parents are coming.

The changes made to the Hungarian adoption system has all but stopped foreigners from adopting Hungarian children (and there weren't many adoptions to begin with.) There just are too many other countries that make it so easy to adopt a child that there is no reason to stay in Hungary for a month. Instead of making the process easier, Hungary is moving to eventually close these large institutions and instead set up a group home system for perhaps 12 children at a time.

That may be better than an institution but it seems to me the best solution would be to make it easier for prospective parents to get over here and take some kids to loving homes.

Every visit, our respect for the women taking care of these children grew along with our frustration with the families that leave these children behind and the government that dooms them to stay. The caregivers are universally excellent, doing so much with so little.

Of course, spending time with Kristiana was great... but I was totally done with being in the orphanage. Every child I met has stolen a piece of my heart, and I didn't have all that many pieces left after three trips there.

It was just overwhelmingly sad to be there. It makes you want to yell at the world about what is happening to the world's children.

But few are listening.

CHAPTER 36: We say goodbye

It was time for yet another farewell at the orphanage (remember my absolute pledge never to attend another one of these?), and I simply cannot tell you how emotional these are. We consider it very lucky that the caregivers here care so much about each child, but it is so hard to say goodbye.

Kim and I had been shuttling back and forth to Budapest from Indiana, taking turns raising our daughter and other kids, as well as trying to stay employed. This trip we should be coming home as a trio.

I shuddered to write down any details of this party, but suffice it to say it was a rerun of the other parties, complete with crying children, crying caregivers, and crying parents. Kristie, on the other hand, was happy as could be, spinning around in her new clothes.

We exchanged her orphanage clothes for store-bought goodies and she was beyond thrilled to be wearing new duds.

After some awful goodbyes we headed off to Budapest on Route 4 to convince the American Embassy to let us go home.

We met with the Embassy doctor (the same guy who did the other five kids), and he gave Kristiana a clean bill of health, so we were ready for the final visa and passport. This time we had all of the paperwork in order, proving that eventually even we can be taught.

The few days of waiting offered us a great chance to do some more sightseeing. My first thought was to drive to Romania or Austria, but without Kristie's passport we could not do that. So we got in the rental car and drove across the Chain Bridge (the oldest bridge across the Danube) and headed up into the Castle district. There we got a close-up look at Buda Castle, finished by St. Stephen in the 17th Century, and the remains of the original castles, one of which was blown up by the Allies in WW II. Today there are archeological digs going on to find the artifacts of the original castles and to restore them.

While at the top of the District, we saw a caravan of Diplomatic Corps Mercedes-Benzes whiz by for a performance of Handel's Messiah in one of the country's oldest and most gorgeous churches. One of the television cameramen there photographed Kristie sitting in her stroller watching the dignitaries arrive in the light drizzle.

After that trip, we ventured back to the hotel for her nap, while I did my MBA homework online.

Kristie was a dream about going to sleep; she would just lie down and drift off in seconds. She woke up periodically and violently rocked her head back and forth to put herself to sleep, which is pretty normal orphanage behavior.

The next day we wandered down a few blocks to the outdoor shopping region and took in some sights as well as wolfed down some pizza, feeding the crusts to the abundant pigeons.

We met our friend Erika in the lobby and then drove across the Danube to the top of a nearby hill, where sits the Hungarian "Statue of Liberty." It's become a tradition for us to stand there with our newly liberated kids as a symbol of, well, *something*. They'll appreciate it someday.

The most overpowering aspect of life here is the amazing, stunning historical buildings and structures here. Some are protected, but Erika notes that new construction tends to be wildly modern because people here are "tired" of so much history. One crumbling castle is being rebuilt into a Four Seasons Hotel.

During Kristie's naptime, I took Erika downstairs to the "Las Vegas Casino" while Kim did some GE work online in the room. I wanted to show Erika the inside of her first casino as well as borrow her language skills. It turned out all betting was done in dollars (the only stable currency.) I started playing blackjack and hit a hot streak. The man next to me (from Argentina) saw my luck and shoved his entire pile of chips into the circle for one bet and won on a 17 to the dealer's bust. I ended up $250 and Erika was up about $25, so that was a nice bonus.

After Kristie's nap, we walked a few blocks to a Hungarian Tex-Mex restaurant (if you can believe there is such a thing) called the Iguana. Kristie was in a grand mood, loving the red neon and colorful walls and charming the waiters as they walked by. All of the sleep must have done her good because she played tickle games and grabbed our fingers to "dance" for about an hour after we returned to the hotel.

One or both of us had been trying for a week to reach the American Embassy, but they didn't seem to care about us or getting us out of there. They don't return phone calls and it's nearly impossible to "drop in." So that was getting increasingly frustrating.

It was nice to have time to see the lovely city, but we wanted to go home.

CHAPTER 37: Homeward Bound

The next morning the three of us went for a long walk along the *Váci Utca*, the main shopping area of Budapest. The stores ranged from kiosks selling dead animals (gutted but complete with hooves) to official stores for Gucci and Nike. There was a bustling crowd, mostly locals because tourism had slowed along with the American economy. I nearly had to slug an overly aggressive portrait artist but otherwise had a good time looking around. I managed to bargain a vendor down 50 percent on a hand-carved chess set for Brandon but didn't buy much else.

Kristiana had been a doll. One night we took in a very good restaurant, and she sat in the high-chair quietly eating chips until the dinner could arrive. She was just amazingly well-behaved and happy. She had bonded strongly with us, which was great. Her blond curls had grown longer, but she resembled "Pebbles" from the Flintstones if you put her hair up.

We piled into a taxi for a ride to the passport office, which also doubles as a license branch, tax office and some sort of welfare office. People were stuffed in this place (waiting in line is a Hungarian tradition) about six deep. I made my way into the office and presented my receipt. The woman remembered me, but asked for my passport, which was downstairs in the waiting taxi. So I trouped down there and brought it back up, only to have the woman nod and not even look at it. ("Papers! I vant to see your papers.")

We then took the same taxi to the American Embassy. We were told to wait outside by the stern guard, so we lounged with the Yugoslavians in a small park across the street. Kristie ran around arms out like Frankenstein trying to catch the pigeons (no dice) and playing with a petulant dog that had arrived with three women.

At the appointed time, we met Maria, a Hungarian who works at the Embassy processing visas. She had processed our other kids, so was pretty familiar with the case. Being American citizens, we were escorted out of the bulletproof waiting area into the plush Americans lounge...*wait, that was a dream*. In fact, we spent the next half-hour shoveling paperwork through the little slot in the bulletproof glass. There's nothing touchy-feely about working with the INS. The system really is impersonal and ugly, like waiting at a Ticketmaster outlet for a Springsteen ticket.

The other people lucky enough to be waiting in the small room with us (five windows for service, no one manning any of them) included a couple of young women trying to get into the USA as *au pairs*, one lithe Hungarian circus performer who had landed a job with Ringling Bros. in Florida, and one frustrated American man trying to determine how to get his newborn son an American passport. (He had a Hungarian wife and was repeatedly told she'd have to wait in Hungary for a couple of years to get to the United States.)

After listening to their stories and many others in the waiting room it was clear the current system (called the "Green Card Lottery") is stupid and antiquated. They ought to scrape the "give me your tired, your hungry" stuff off the American Statue of Liberty because there's no good way to immigrate to the United States legally.

Kim took the baby back to the hotel (about a six block walk), and I waited around for the visa to be completed, which took another hour. During that time, the line outside (mostly Yugoslavians) grew larger, and I got to see first-hand some pretty impressive scenes. (Obviously, there is no American Embassy left in Yugoslavia, so Budapest is the closest one). One young couple received their visas and the woman openly wept as she carefully wrapped them in an old plastic bag.

I finally got our visa shoved through the slot and went back to the hotel before Kristie fell asleep.

Kim and I spent the next hour looking at our paperwork, counting documents and assuring we were ready to go home. She packed up our stuff, and I called the airlines trying to get out. We lucked out and found a flight out the next morning at 7 A.M.

We woke up at 4 A.M. and ran out to the rental car, filling it to bulging with all of our junk. We passed both immigration and security screens at Ferihegy Airport in Budapest with no issues whatsoever and made it onto the half-empty plane with time to spare.

Once again we had opted not to buy a seat for Kristie, but no matter -- we had entire aisles of the plane to ourselves.

I would love to tell you another horror story about the plane ride home, but this one was a dream. Two parents, one happy baby and plenty of room to stretch out. (Dad used real juice in her bottles this time... no projectile vomiting.) I actually slept some on this flight, stretched out across five seats.

After landing in New York, we cleared customs and the still-surly INS office, then boarded the connecting flight to home. In Evansville, we were mobbed at the airport by our other children, Kim's parents and a couple of friends. The other kids hugged Kristie, who looked more than a little overwhelmed by the whole thing.

As we sat on the airport carpeting watching our daughter play with her siblings, both Kim and I were weeping.

We'd done it. And we hoped we were done.

CHAPTER 38: We're done, I think

Kristie adjusted to life at home almost immediately. Ava eventually quit thinking she was her doll, and life went on as planned, including the seemingly required trip to Dr. Logan for tonsils and ear tubes.

Shortly after we got home, we got a call from a producer at "The Today Show" asking if they could go on summer vacation with us. That was the same summer Kim and I got a 30-foot RV and decided to show our kids "real America." Like idiots we said yes, so that summer we were followed all over America by NBC News, which aired a nice four-minute segment on us in early September 2001.

(They nicely didn't include in the final piece that we lost Adam in the crowd at the Lincoln Memorial during a particularly hectic part of the journey.)

Oooops.

We saw so many neat things on that trip and learned so much about our kids. (And learned a lot about how to sleep 10 people in an RV.)

When we went to a Six Flags outside Washington, DC we were greeted by guards with metal detectors, not something we normally see in Indiana's friendly theme parks.

"Dad, why are they searching everyone?" Brandon asked.

"Because this is the murder capital of America," I replied.

He got wide eyes and said, "Six Flags is the murder capital of America?"

Riding the log-plume ride with Willie and Brandon, we got absolutely, positively, squishy-underpants drenched. Adam, who was watching on the sidelines, freaked the first time he saw us go under the plume, which issues a huge "whomp" of water upon impact. He thought we were all dead.

Back to losing Adam…

The next morning we were to meet the Today Show crew (a producer, soundman, cameraman and reporter Bob Dotson) at Arlington National Cemetery, the permanent resting place of 275,000 American servicemen and their dependents. Thinking "how hard could 5,000 acres of cemetery be to find?" we left the campground at 8:30 for our 10 A.M. appointment.

Turns out, of course, that all of Maryland and Virginia was under construction. We spent most of the time in bumper-to-bumper traffic. Complicating matters was that there was no signage in either state. There were NO billboards thanks to state law, which is a good thing…the highways are gorgeous. However, it is amazing anyone can be buried at Arlington because *no one can find it.*

We find ourselves behind the Pentagon, which interested me because *I had no idea the Pentagon was in Virginia.* So I hung a left and discovered we were on the Roosevelt Bridge heading into the heart of Downtown Washington in a 35-foot motor-home. I was trying not to get us killed when I noticed a guy frantically pointing to the rear of the RV as he passed me. So I pulled over and discovered I had a flat rear tire.

Does it get any better than this?

Kim got on the cell phone with the Today Show people, who are wondering where we are. Because I had four rear tires, I elected to continue slowly back to Virginia over another bridge. Miraculously I found myself so close to Arlington that I saw the tombstones. I could look out one window and see the Iwo Jima Memorial and look out the other and see the U.S. Marine Corps Memorial.

Despite being able to **SEE** the cemetery and between us holding four college degrees, we could not find a way in. So we parked in sight of these two monuments and waited for help. As I considered setting the RV ablaze to alert someone, we got an escort to lead us to the entrance.

We met Bob Dotson, producer Laurie Singer, and the two crewmen. They could not have been nicer about the flat tire. A few minutes later a tire man arrived from AAA; he would have dressed better had he known repairing my tire would garner network news coverage.

Once we got the tire repaired, Kim and I were "miked" under our shirts, and the sound man and cameraman got in the RV with us and filmed from the inside as we drove across the Memorial Bridge to the Lincoln Memorial. I then dropped everyone off and drove the RV by myself to the only spot we could reserve to park a large RV, at the National Gallery about 10 miles away.

While I was driving there and taking a cab back, Kim met with the crew, and Kristie was walking Edit up and down the 1,000 steps to the top of the Lincoln Memorial and back. Adam became entranced with Abe Lincoln (the marble version) sitting in his chair. He just found the stony Abe fascinating.

When I arrived to the utter chaos of the moment, the NBC crew jumped back to work, filming us walking around. Kim suggested I take a moment and go to the top to view Abe for myself because I had missed it earlier. I did so, with Brandon, Ava, and Willie in tow. I then took the three kids down the steps and joined Kim at the base as we started to walk to the Vietnam Memorial.

We raised our fingers as we always do, counting off how many of the little kids each of us has under their control. I raised three fingers; Kim raised three.

She stopped cold and said, "Where's Adam?"

We looked around. It turns out the sound man had been holding Adam's hand but just dropped it and went back to work when I arrived. (Obviously not a parent.)

We frantically called for him among the 1,000 people milling around. After a couple awful minutes (only a parent can feel that terror of a missing kid in a huge crowd), Kim said she bet he was back up top with old Abe. I sprinted up the steps about 10 at a time, noticing the NBC cameraman was keeping up with me stride for stride, his camera trained on me the whole time.

At the top I swept through the right side of the monument and found nothing but throngs of Boy Scouts. I ran though the middle, also nothing. On the left side, to my audible relief, I saw Adam leaning against the wall, watching old Abe. I grabbed him as the cameraman zoomed in. Adam didn't seem upset at first and I thought maybe we were not going to be on the Today Show as the world's worst parents. A couple seconds later he leaned into my chest (where my wireless mic was) and said, "Why did you and mommy leave me for so long?"

Sigh.

We feel terrible about it still but it was a scary experience that I guess happens to everyone. We were lucky they cut it out of the piece.

Adam was obsessed with Abe Lincoln from then on, continually jabbering about wanting a photo of him to hold. Not being near a computer or a darkroom I had nothing much to offer him. Totally exasperated by the end of the day, I ended up giving Adam a five-dollar bill and a penny, which made him very pleased to have two images of Abe to look at.

(Adam insisted at one point on the trip that we had to go back to the Memorial and "chip off the stone so Abe Lincoln can walk and talk" and so he can "get up out of the chair.")

Ava, on the other hand, continually referred to the Statue of Liberty as the "Statue of Barbie."

Little things like that just warm our hearts.

Walking around the Statue of Liberty and Ellis Island Kim and I couldn't help but think of how lucky our new children are. She and I talked amid the chaos of keeping everyone together on the Ellis Island tour, of how our adoption adventure had forever changed our family tree. Our struggle was not nearly that of most of those at Ellis Island but it was easy to see the connection as you walked through the exhibits trailed by six little immigrants from Hungary.

We toured Washington, Philadelphia, and New York, among many other places along the way. We showed the kids what it was like to live together in close quarters, how campfires work, and how to empty the holding tanks in an RV. (Stand way back, pull the lever and run!)

We got to ride in a limo in Manhattan, take in Times Square and walk around the World Trade Center Plaza.

We had no way of knowing a month later it would be gone.

When people hear that my husband, Jim, and I adopted six children from Hungary, they nearly always question our sanity. When they find out we did it while helping my 17-year-old daughter choose a college, they become convinced we are certifiably crazy.

"You're almost finished," they say. "Why would you want to go through all that again? Remember dirty diapers? Remember temper tantrums? Remember not being able to go out as a couple without enlisting help from the National Guard?"

But the joys Jim and I have experienced with our two children from previous marriages are among the reasons we were convinced it was worth starting over. Another aspect was the opportunity to raise children together.

Adopting internationally — especially older children — is not something anyone should be "talked into." Jim and I made a pact long ago that we'd only accept an adoption referral if we both were 100 percent behind it. And I must admit, when the kids are running circles around us screaming, it's great for each of us to know we went into this with our best friend.

When we first told family and friends about our plan, several expressed concern that it would interfere with our closeness as a couple. Any parent knows that is a valid concern, so on the plane to Hungary, we committed to making sure we would make time for each other.

While it's not always easy, especially around the holidays, we are taking great care to maintain our closeness. We are committed to providing our children with an example of a loving, respectful and emotionally healthy relationship.

We've been humbled by so many things since we met our children. The feeling first came over us when we read the references written by several of our friends for the home study that is required of potential adoptive parents.

That feeling returns daily as our friends and family display their support for our decision. We also feel it each time we're fortunate enough to catch the look of wonder that spreads across the faces of our children with every new "first." It doesn't seem to matter whether it is the first time they are allowed to play with raindrops or the first time they spy a house decorated with Christmas lights; so many things fill them with awe.

We're humbled each night as we go from one bedroom to the next to untangle their legs from around the toys they've slipped into bed. Jim will make me smile by saying in a stage whisper, "There's two more in here," as he kneels beside the next bed to kiss yet another sleeping child.

Every family that has adopted an older child has gone through several months of challenging behavior as the child adapted to his new surroundings. Our family has been no exception. How many of us could pack up our belongings, go with people we've only known for a few weeks (and can't understand) to live in a world full things we'd never even imagined?

Even though we've been around many toddlers, it helped when we started seeking out other parents and comparing notes. I must admit I've been tickled to discover there are plenty of children who make the live wrecking balls at our house appear angelic: "So Johnny threw your watch down the toilet? I'm so glad to hear that!"

Even though the list of things that need to be repaired because of the children is two pages long and growing, I think most of our challenges are related more to "normal" attempts by toddlers to assert their own independence than to the adoption or culture shock.

For their first two months in America, neither Kristian nor Willie seemed willing to let us out of their sight. They seemed particularly starved for male attention (presumably because all the people in the orphanage except two were female).

They literally would attach themselves to Jim's legs when he'd walk in the door, and they would refuse to let go. If I managed to detach one of them in hopes of helping Jim get into the house, it would set off a tantrum that would continue until bedtime. I'd go for the other boy, only to have the first one reattach himself.

There comes a time every night when Jim or I try to say something to the other above the chaotic din, only to realize that we can barely hear ourselves, much less the other person. When the realization hits, we look at each other, then at the bouncing, running, often screaming bundles of energy who are our children, and we shake our heads.

Almost always a laugh follows; sometimes it comes from the tips of our toes, other times there's a rueful ring to it. But whatever the ups and downs of the moment, I can look at him and know that we're all in it together.

We've become a family.

EPILOGUE

Today, Coleen is married and living a successful life with her husband, Clint, in Indianapolis.

Brandon is 14 and an honor student. He made fast friends with his little brothers and sisters, and I hope the experience of going from an only child to the biggest boy wasn't too traumatic. He loves playing the sax and will be driving soon (!).

Kristian, 13, also an honor-roll student, is our poster-child for the benefits of adopting older children; his transition from waif to young man was dramatic and quick. If anything needs to be done or anyone needs help, Kristian is there. He's quickly mastering the trombone.

Willie, 12, is working hard to overcome his challenges. He is a very good-hearted boy, loving and tender at all the right times. With a great team of teachers, Will is progressing academically at a good pace. Thanks to a gluten-free, casein-free, dairy-free and sugar-free diet lovingly prepared by his mother, we've seen great progress in his autism as well.

Adam, 9, was born to play baseball. We don't know how or why (he never saw a game in the orphanage) but he loves playing the game. We often find him asleep in his bed wearing a hat and mitt or holding a ball. He loves his Cub Scout activities and playing outside.

Twin sister Ava, 9, is our fashion plate. She has the "hip" gene and uses it to her advantage. (Mom and I were able to dangle the prospect of pierced ears before Ava in exchange for months of good behavior.) She is first with a hug and loves animals. She's also a good writer and may write the sequel to this book someday.

Cary, 8, adjusted to the family quickly and shares his sister's fashion sense. (He's often dressed better than I am.) He loves art, music, video games and puppies. He loves cars, especially PT Cruisers. (We bought one to make him happy.)

Kristiana, 6, is a classic beauty with the Hungarian gene of stubbornness thrown in. We needn't have worried about bringing a little girl into the mix as the last child. She loves all things Barbie and pink.

**Brandon, Kristian, Willie, Adam, Ava,
Cary and Kristie at Coleen's wedding, 2004**

As for mom and dad, we're frazzled but alive. Some days our calendars have to be orchestrated like a moon launch, but we do our best to get the kids to every event and save a little time for us. Usually the "us" time is what has to go but that's what retirement is for, I guess.

When people ask me "how do you do it?" I always have the same answer: "I married well."

Professionally, Kim remains communications manager at GE Plastics in Mount Vernon, Indiana.

I joined GE in 2000 as a leader in Information Technology. I completed my MBA in April 2005 and also launched a national business repairing computers (www.cyberdads.com). There's a lot going on, but we pledged to pay off our last child before the first hit college.

As for adoption, we are hearing from many other couples that the process is much better now than when we first got into the game. We're also hearing the INS is now much easier to work with since it was taken over by the Department of Homeland Security and basically slapped around. I hope that is true.

Financially it is much easier now to adopt. There are huge tax credits for adopting children both from the United States and overseas ($10,630 per child) as well as ongoing support if you adopt children with some special needs. Many companies offer adoption assistance programs. The E.W. Scripps Co., where I used to work, offered us $4,000 per child when we adopted our first four children; General Electric offered couples $2,000 per child then.

So don't let financial needs get in the way of giving a child a home. Just visit with a child in foster care or in a group home, and you will walk away with the goal of doing anything you can to get them out of there and into a loving home.

Our advice remains the same as Nike's when it comes to adoption.

Just do it.

ACKNOWLEDGEMENTS

There are so many people to thank for our adoption experiences and for helping us through.

---To my beloved Kimberly: I never would have dreamed life with my best friend would be so crowded.

I set out on a narrow way many years ago

Hoping I would find true love along the broken road

But I got lost a time or two

Wiped my brow and kept pushing through

I couldn't see how every sign pointed straight to you.

Every long lost dream led me to where you are

Others who broke my heart, they were like northern stars

Pointing me on my way, into your loving arms

This much I know is true:

That God blessed the broken road

That led me straight to you

---To Edit Ferenc: We could not have done any of this without you. Our children had love in their life when they needed it most. Thank you for being part of our family. We love you.

---To Coleen: Thank you for letting me into your life. I am so impressed with the young woman you have become.

---To Brandon: Thank you for stepping up and agreeing to give up your relative peace for this ruckus. You have been a good brother and, more importantly, a fine son. *I'll love you forever, I'll like you for always; forever and ever my baby you'll be.*

---To my Six-Pack: Kristian, William, Adam, Ava, Cary, and Kristiana: You are a light of my life and the capstone of my years on Earth. *Thanks for giving me at least a fighting chance to be your dad.*

---To my parents, Walter and Jean Elaine: Thank you for supporting our decisions and for being there for us. *I miss you, Mom.*

---To Kim's parents, Dan and JoAnn: Thank you for your support and for holding down the fort more than once.

---To Harold and Darla Grossman: Thank you for following your dream and for liberating little Leila and for being our friends.

---To János: Thank you for your expertise and for doing everything you said you would exactly on time.

---To my brother Tim and sister Nancy: We are family: Thank you for everything.

---To our friends, among them Linda & Dave, Steve & Terri, Mim & Doug, Kay & Keith, Ron & Kim, Donna, Beth & Dan, Sherry, Roseann: Thank you for being there. (Feel free to baby-sit.)

---To our extended family, including the Burkes (especially Dick, Barbara and Arlene), the Wolffs, the Jacobses, and the Derks: We need you more every day.

---To our doctors, including Dr. Thomas Logan, Dr. Louis Cady, and Dr. Jim Jenison. Thanks for caring for our children like they were your own.

---To our too numerous GE friends, including Hutch, Ashley, Jeff, Thad, Charlie, Bob, Les, and the many others who have helped pick up the slack when we needed it. Thank you.

---To Tom Tuley: Thank you for my first break.

And to the readers who have now shared our joy.

APPENDIX: Adoption Resources

We've been asked for a lot of advice over the years on how to adopt, where to adopt and how to keep the process sane. In the Internet age, the goal is research. Know everything there is to know about your country and research it extensively.

Adopt US Kids

http://www.adoptuskids.org

If this Web site had been around when we started the process we likely would have adopted within the United States.

The U.S. Citizenship and Immigration Service

http://uscis.gov/graphics/

U.S. Guidelines for Adoption

http://uscis.gov/graphics/services/index2.htm

Country-Specific Adoption Rules

http://travel.state.gov/family/adoption/country/country_369.html

What you will find on this site is the specific rules to adopt in the country you choose. For example, the current rules in Hungary require, as initial paperwork,

DOCUMENTS REQUIRED
FOR ADOPTION IN HUNGARY:

In order to be placed on the national register of adoptive parents, the following documents must be submitted:

- *Home study performed by a U.S. licensed agency or a social worker;*
- *Proof of income of adoptive parents;*
- *Psychological evaluation of adoptive parents;*
- *Advance approval of foreign state, i.e. official notification of I-600A approval;*
- *Certificate of citizenship;*
- *Statement of adoptive parents regarding motivation for adoption and expectations about the child;*
- *Adoptive parents' statements consenting to their registration on the national register;*
- *License of adoption agency, if applicable.*

Adoption Law

http://uscis.gov/graphics/services/appen.htm

Hungary Adoption Facilitator

Ours was East-West Concepts

www.eastwestconcepts.com

Adoption Agency

Although we did not use an agency, we endorse and recommend Families Thru International Adoption for adoptions from many countries other than Hungary, including China and Russia.

www.ftia.org

ABOUT THE AUTHOR

James Derk, a native of Chicago, has been honored with more than 40 journalism awards, including News Writer of the Year for Scripps Howard Newspapers. In his 17-year newspaper career he became a specialist in First Amendment issues and aviation and was one of the first reporters to practice "computer-assisted reporting."

He holds a Bachelor of Science degree in Journalism from Southern Illinois University in Carbondale, a certificate in management from the University of Southern Indiana and an MBA from the University of Phoenix.

He currently serves as IT Leader for GE Plastics and is co-owner of CyberDads (www.cyberdads.com) a national computer repair firm.

A dedicated community volunteer, he is chairman of GE Volunteers in the Ohio Valley, chairman of the IT Alliance at the School of Business at the University of Southern Indiana and assistant Cubmaster for Cub Scout Pack 305 in Newburgh, Indiana.

Printed in the United States
61063LVS00002B/152

9 781425 957124